WILLIAM CAREY: BY TRADE A COBBLER

William Carey:
By Trade a Cobbler

KELLSYE M. FINNIE

Illustrations by John Finnie

STL BOOKS
BROMLEY, KENT
KINGSWAY PUBLICATIONS
EASTBOURNE

ISBN (Kingsway) 0 86065 437 0
ISBN (STL) 1 85078 011 0

Unless otherwise indicated biblical quotations are from the
Authorized version (Crown copyright)

STL Books are published by Send the Light
(Operation Mobilisation), P.O. Box 48, Bromley,
Kent, England.

Front cover photo: The Photo Source

Printed in Great Britain for
KINGSWAY PUBLICATIONS LTD
Lottbridge Drove, Eastbourne, E. Sussex BN23 6NT by
Cox & Wyman Ltd, Reading.
Typeset by Nuprint Services Ltd, Harpenden, Herts.

Contents

Foreword

On any showing, William Carey was one of God's very great servants. His dedication to God and to the missionary task was total. His gifts as pioneer, linguist, botanist were unusually rich. His achievements were astonishing and their results are still to be seen a century and a half after his death.

His story deserves to be told again. There are several biographies but I welcome this short one by Kellsye Finnie. Its brevity will bring it within the reach of many who would not read the longer books. Its vividness of style will, I hope, catch the imagination of many who previously have known little, if anything, of this man.

In the background of this book is the tragic figure of the hero's wife, itself raising grave questions in the minds of those concerned with missionary service. But above all there is the picture of absolute dedication on the part of William Carey to the cause of the propagation of the gospel and of his devotion to Christ.

May this book catch the imagination and touch the conscience of many readers.

DONALD COGGAN

Acknowledgements

I am indebted to earlier biographers of Carey,
notably F. Deauville Walker and S. Pearce Carey.
Also to Colin Ellis who wrote the volume entitled
History in Leicester.

I am also grateful to the Baptist Missionary Society,
the *Northampton Mercury*, Leicester City Reference
Library and the Leicester City Records Office, for
help in research.

Up-to-date information has been provided by the
Rev. J. K. Skirrow, a BMS missionary at Serampore
College, and the Carey Museum in Serampore.

Prologue

The picture is of William Carey (1761–1834), missionary pioneer.

The glass through which we see the picture is the England of stage coaches, small provincial towns and tiny isolated villages.

There were few schools and many illiterate people. Slave traffic, fear of disease and poverty were subjects never far from the minds of the country folk.

A small land set in a vast world, it provided little opportunity for travel. But many people became aware of other lands as news filtered through to the villages. They heard of the exciting explorations of Captain Cook, and of war in Canada, America and the West Indies.

The solid frame holding the picture is made up of the memory of men like Andrew Fuller, John Sutcliff, Dr Ryland, Robert Hall, Marshman, Ward and others. Holding the picture for ever on the walls of missionary enterprise is the silver cord woven by the prayers of the people of Carey's day.

Glossary

Pundit:	Hindu learned in Sanskrit and philosophy, religion and science of India.
Sanskrit:	The ancient and sacred language of India.
Shastra:	A sacred Hindu writing.
Sati:	Custom requiring a Hindu woman to sacrifice herself on her husband's funeral pyre.
Hook-swinging:	An Indian custom of self-torture.
Flitting:	Old Northamptonshire word for moving house.
Dissenter:	Member of a sect that has separated itself from the Church of England.
Palanquin:	Covered litter used in India and the East.
Pukka:	Anglo-Indian word meaning permanent—solidly built.
Venetian window:	Window with three separate openings.

I

'It's a Boy!'

The little village of Paulerspury in Northamptonshire was quiet in the sunshine of an August day in 1761. In the small thatched cottage of Edmund and Elizabeth Carey there was not even the usual monotonous thudding of the loom which stood in the window of the largest room. The weaver had no heart for work today and he sat at the open door.

But there was a bustle of activity going on in the tiny bedroom above. He could hear the busy footsteps of his mother and a nurse as they tended his wife.

At last, the waiting man heard the faint sound of a baby's cry, followed by the words of the older woman.

'It's a boy! We will call the precious child William.'

Some time later, wrapped in the shawl she had made, the baby was carried in her arms to the window, looking out at the high, square tower of the parish church at the top of the hill.

'God has been good to me,' she whispered. 'He has given me my first grandchild.'

The gentle grandmother lived here in this home,

and added her influence to the love, piety, church going and Bible reading that enfolded the child in an atmosphere of peace as he grew.

William's father, though a weaver by trade, was a man of some education. Six years later he was asked to become the new schoolmaster of Paulerspury, a position his father had held before him. This meant moving into the schoolhouse, so the family prepared for what was commonly called 'a flitting'. Tables, chairs and beds were stacked outside the cottage on the hill.

Carefully, the small boy carried his case of insects and his birds in their home-made cage, treasures too precious to be entrusted to anyone else. He left these in the new home while he returned to fetch the plants he had been growing in the old garden. Flowers and trees, plants, birds and insects were his passions. His understanding parents allowed him to turn his bedroom at the schoolhouse into a miniature museum.

Each time he went out into the lanes nearby he was on the lookout for some new thing to add to his collection.

But he also had time for play, and his favourite game at that time was climbing trees with his companions. Often he would crawl up into the lofty branches higher than was safe, urging his friends to follow him. Rarely were they able to pass him.

One day the inevitable happened, and William was badly injured in the fall. But as soon as he recovered, and was well enough to go out, he tried the same difficult climb again, and this time he managed it! This determination in his spirit was a sore trial to his mother's peace of mind, but it was to stand him in good stead in later life. Many were the trees of adversity and difficulty he attempted time after time, where a weaker spirit might have been tempted to give in.

William tackled the art of learning to read with the same zest, and quickly mastered it. Books became another passion and he read all he could find. From the start he had a hungry mind for learning, and news of the outside world which filtered slowly through to the village roused his keenest interest.

The *Northampton Mercury* was one of the earliest weekly papers. It was published each Monday, giving national and foreign news, and three copies found their way to Paulerspury. One for the squire, one for the rector and the other copy for the schoolmaster. A never-failing thrill and excitement attended the arrival of this weekly paper. All who could read waited their turn to borrow one of the copies, while a cluster of illiterate neighbours gathered round to listen. Eagerly, the latest news was then discussed in the cottages.

There were items to delight the heart of any boy. Wonderful stories of the power of James Watt's steam engine, something alive and vibrating. There was Arkwright's new spinning machine, an invention that brought a worried frown to the brow of the weavers, fearing the loss of their living.

When Carey was eleven the *Mercury* became full of the topic of the hour—slavery. He read it all, and immediately his interest and sympathy were aroused. He felt a concern which never left him for the rest of his life.

When he and his friends heard of the Boston Tea Riots in 1773 they found a new impetus for their games of soldiers, and fighting on the village green. This was something like excitement!

One day, in his search for a book to read, William

found in the schoolhouse a volume about botany, a subject after his own heart. But the words baffled him. Eventually, he took the book to Thomas Jones, a weaver in the village who had the reputation of knowing a great deal about words.

'Please, can you tell me what these names mean?' he asked, when Jones answered the urgent knocking on his door. He took the book from under his arm and opened it out on the cottage table. Jones looked at it with growing surprise.

'It is little wonder you cannot understand these words, boy. They are written in the Latin tongue!'

'But, sir, can you not tell me what they mean?'

'Yes indeed, I can and I will, my boy. When I was young my father sent me to Kidderminster Grammar School, hoping to make me a doctor. There I learnt, among other things, to read Latin, but I was idle and eventually I threw away my chances. So you see me now, just a poor weaver. But my memory is good and you too have a memory and a mind to learn. Sit down here and one day, please God, you too will understand and read the Latin language.'

William had started on his conquest of foreign languages and he proved a quick learner. His appetite was insatiable and before long he was also studying Greek.

Now Carey was seldom seen without a book. Science, travel and history he devoured with relish. Often his friends would come across him lying in a corner of the village green, lost to the world as his active mind thrilled to the pictures conjured up by the words he was reading.

'Here's Columbus!' they called to one another. 'Off

on his travels again!' He was so absorbed their com-
ments had no power to interrupt him.

2

'In Service for Jesus Christ'

When schooldays were over, William's ambition was to earn his living by working as a gardener among the plants he loved. He tried this for a time, but his sensitive skin was quickly irritated by the sun as he toiled in the open air. Sadly, he realized he must set his mind to a different career.

His father then apprenticed him to a shoemaker, Clarke Nicholls of Piddington, a village nine miles away. Here he learnt a new trade, making the good shoes that were needed in an age when walking was often the only means of getting from one place to another. Although he didn't realize it at the time, his own feet were here being 'fitted with the readiness that comes from the gospel of peace' (Ephesians 6:15, New International Version).

There was one other apprentice in the workshop at Piddington. Thomas Warr was the son of a Dissenter (a person who had left the Established Church), and as he and William worked together they talked. Often they argued about their differing views on church doctrine. With his mastery of words Carey could easily disarm the less scholarly Warr. But strangely his triumphs brought him no lasting satisfaction. There was something about the faith of his workmate that was personal and real, an unmistakable 'something' that went far beyond mere head knowledge.

Since a child the Bible had been an open book to William. He had heard it read in church, and daily in his parents' home. It was part of his background and he had accepted its teaching in much the same way as his daily food. He believed it all but in his discussions with Warr he began to see that in his own experience there was something lacking. Formal acceptance of the Christian faith was not enough, but would need to give place to a definite heart acceptance. He needed a personal encounter with Christ as Saviour before Christ could become Lord of his life. Restless and unhappy, he longed for the peace that eluded him, yet he was not ready to take the step of absolute commitment.

In 1779 there was a national crisis. The American War was dragging on and England was also at war with France and Spain. English soldiers were fighting in India. At home, families were divided and hearts were sad and bewildered. The King called for a National Day of Prayer, and this was arranged for February 10th.

For this Warr invited Carey to accompany him to the Meeting House at Shackleton. On the Day of Prayer they hurried through their shoemaking, and early in the evening went together to join the prayer group in the Dissenters' small room.

One of the members read a verse from Hebrews 13:

'Let us go forth therefore unto him without the camp, bearing his reproach' (v.13). The words were familiar to William but this time they reached down deep into his heart. There must be a personal involvement, a willingness to bear the reproach of Christ in a world that still rejected him. As the meeting continued William made the decision to commit his life to Christ, his intellectual belief giving place to heart surrender.

This was not a blinding flash on a Damascus Road, but a slow and gradual reaching out after weeks of earnest seeking, realizing at last that it was Christ who had found him, granting him the peace that passes understanding.

Now he turned to the Bible with a new interest. During his growing years he had come up against a diversity of teaching, but now he settled down to an intensive study of the book that could give him the guidance he needed. His aim was to be in service for Jesus Christ, to preach the gospel, to carry out the divine duty of calling men to Christ.

His circumstances did nothing to help him at this time. The shoemaker, Clarke Nicholls, was taken ill and died during the year, thus the apprenticeship was never completed. Carey went to work as a journeyman shoemaker with Mr Old of Hackleton, making shoes and then travelling round to take them to the customers. Because his experience of the trade was so limited his wages were on a pitifully low scale.

There were, however, periods of pleasant sailing as well as the rough seas. For some time he had been 'walking out' with the young sister-in-law of his employer. Dorothy Placket's father was one of the elders at the Meeting House and this was where he met her. She was a shy country maid with little education but William loved her for her gentle nature. In his eyes she was as beautiful as the Helen he came across in his Greek readings.

But as yet he was not sure of Dorothy's feelings for him, or whether she would be willing to marry him. As they walked home one Sunday evening he determined to ask the question uppermost in his mind.

'Dorothy, will you marry me?'

She looked startled. 'Oh! William! But are you sure you want to marry *me*? You know I'm not a scholar and your books don't speak to me as they do to you. I can't even read them!'

Gently he turned her to face him: 'But, Dorothy, do you love me?' he persisted.

Already he saw the happiness in her lovely eyes and he knew the answer.

'Yes, William, I do. I love you dearly,' she whispered.

He held her close: 'Then that is enough. Perhaps I couldn't teach the love to grow in your heart were it not there already. But I *can* teach you to read. I can, Dorothy! I can and I will. You shall see!'

He was twenty when they married in June 1781. Their cottage home in Hackleton was small but neat. For added joy there was a garden where William cultivated his plants and flowers.

He and Dorothy grew closer in their grief when their first child died before she reached the age of two. Although there were to be more children, these could never entirely take the place of the little girl they lost.

3

Shoemaker and Schoolmaster

In the early part of the 18th century the spiritual and
moral tone of the country was low. Indifference pre-
dominated and religious observance had become a
mere formality. Then came the evangelical revival led
by John and Charles Wesley and George Whitefield.
It swept through the land with a purifying influence.
By 1775 the Methodist Societies had something like
45,000 members.

Wesley had preached in Carey's neighbourhood on
several occasions and he referred to the congregation
in those villages as: '...the flower of our Societies in
the circuit, both for zeal and simplicity.' The young
William must have known of the services Wesley
conducted and, with his enquiring mind, might well
have gone to listen.

About this time there was also a notable stirring in
the spiritual life among the Nonconformists in
Northamptonshire. Inspired by the writings of the
American Jonathan Edwards, the ministers of
Northamptonshire and surrounding counties formed

themselves into an Association of fellowship and Christian service. At their meeting in 1784 they passed a resolution to establish regular meetings to pray for revival of the churches and for the spread of the gospel. Many of these meetings were held on the first Monday evening of each month. Now other churches joined in, and the wave of prayer which continued under the leadership of men like John Sutcliff became the power house God used to move the churches to support the growing missionary enterprise.

In 1782 Carey had walked over to Olney to attend one of the meetings of the Association, and from that day his life was vitally linked with three other members, John Sutcliff, John Ryland and Andrew Fuller.

He sometimes walked the five miles into Northampton to hear the well-known preacher, Dr Ryland, but more often he went to Olney where the Rev. Thomas Scott had come to live. Years later he wrote of the help he received from this ministry.

'If there be anything of the work of God in my soul, I owe much of it to his preaching when I first set out in the ways of the Lord.'

Friends from the village of Earls Barton invited him to preach for them at their Meeting House and he accepted. Thus began a fortnightly engagement that lasted for three and a half years, and meant an arduous walk of twelve miles each time. It also involved much study. One book which helped him greatly was *Help to Zion's Travellers* by Robert Hall, the famous preacher from Arnesby in Leicestershire. Carey said: 'I do not remember ever to have read any book with such raptures as I did that.' This was indeed high praise from one who loved books more than his daily food.

His conquest of languages continued, and he added Hebrew, Italian, Dutch and French to his studies. His diligence was phenomenal with the compelling force behind all his efforts being the desire to become an efficient and acceptable preacher of the gospel. Such a message, he realized, demanded most careful preparation and was worthy of the highest standard available. With determination he mastered each difficulty and obstacle, and when he looked back in old age he said: 'If anyone should think it worth his while to write my life, if he give me credit for being a plodder he will describe me justly. I can plod. I can persevere in any definite pursuit. To this I owe everything.'

As Carey continued his preaching at Barton he was surprised to have another call that came from Paulerspury, his home village. A handful of people were meeting regularly for Bible study and they wanted him to come to them once a month to preach. He accepted their invitation and the ten mile walk there served two purposes. It was an opportunity to preach to Dissenters, and after the service a chance to visit his parents and family who were opposed to Dissenters! His father was a parish clerk and a devout Anglican and it was unthinkable for him to go to hear William. At the same time he was gratified when he heard neighbours say that his son preached acceptably!

William studied the New Testament, feeling his way in matters of doctrine, and he was willing to act on whatever new light came to him. Although he had been baptized as an infant, he now felt a desire to make a public confession as an adult. He went to see Dr Ryland in Northampton to discuss this with him. The doctor patiently explained that baptism by immersion is a confession of one's faith in Christ, signifying the fact of dying with him and being raised again in new life.

On October 5th, 1783 William was baptized by John Ryland. There was no heated baptistry for this but the cold waters of the River Nen at Northampton, just below the ruined walls of the castle. In later years the river was deviated from its course and the place was made into a railway goods station, where mighty engines came to rest. Their power was but as smoke in contrast to the power of God on which Carey rested, and it was on the promise of that power that he went forward along the path of God's calling.

Life was not easy. The fever which caused the death of his child had attacked him also, and left a legacy of weariness and a distressing cough. Then his employer, Mr Old, became ill and died, leaving William to continue the business alone. He trudged from place to place, selling the shoes he had made and then carrying home a fresh supply of leather for the new ones he must start to make as soon as possible. It left little time for leisure or rest.

Thinking to improve matters he moved his home to a cottage in Piddington, but this proved to be a mistake. The house was not well sited and in wet weather the surrounding land became flooded. It was so damp that William's cough grew even worse, but with dogged determination he mustered his strength and opened a room in his home as a night school for village children. This added financial help to his inadequate income.

Though circumstances were difficult, they were not

allowed to interfere with his personal study, and in the light of his rush lamp Carey would sit for many late hours plodding at his books, a student with an insatiable appetite for learning as well as teaching.

In 1785 Carey heard that the schoolmaster had moved away from the village of Moulton, which was about eleven miles away. This seemed to him an opportunity to improve his condition and he applied for the vacant position.

He was accepted, and on Lady Day he moved his little family once more, this time to Moulton, with its quaint stone cottages and tiny windows peeping through the thatch. In one of these thatched cottages he opened his school and his shoemaker's shop.

4

The Missionary Call

Near the cottage in Moulton stood a small Baptist
Church, and although William was still a member of
the Hackleton Meeting House, he was interested. The
people in the Baptist Church were interested in him
too, and eventually they enlisted his help in their
services. They had no pastor and they knew Carey was
a preacher.

When he finally decided to cast in his lot with the
Baptists, he presented himself as a candidate for
membership to the Church Meeting at Olney. He was
invited to preach there, but it was not until a year later
that they recorded their satisfaction with his ability as
a minister.

In their records it says: 'On August 10th, 1786,
Carey was accepted to preach wherever God in His
providence might call him.' Not in their wildest dreams
could these cautious, devout elders have visualized the
vast area this was to cover!

In November, Moulton formally invited him to
become their minister. The following August he was

ordained there by Ryland, Fuller and Sutcliff, the three men he had met at Olney four years before.

On Carey's 'confession of faith', which was considered 'sound and sensible', he became a fully recognized Baptist Minister. It was a wonderful day for Carey, clouded only by the absence of the mother he loved dearly and who had died a few weeks earlier.

The pastoral office was to him the highest honour on earth. He said: 'Preaching, though a great part, is not all of our employ. We must maintain the character of teacher, bishop, overlooker in the chimney-corner as well as in the pulpit.' In his own chimney-corner one of the rewards of his faithfulness the following October was confirmed in the baptism of his wife.

His financial position was not materially changed for the church could only afford a maximum salary of twelve pounds annually. He received also a yearly sum of five pounds from a central fund in London, making a total of five shillings and ninepence per week, which had to be augmented by his teaching and shoemaking.

His own thirst for knowledge made Carey an ideal teacher. He made the lessons come alive for the boys in his school. For geography classes he pasted together sheets of paper to make a large map and transformed the lessons into a delight, taking his students with him on imaginary journeys into far distant countries.

One day he saw an advertisement in the *Northampton Mercury* for a world globe. What a help one of these would be to his boys! Alas, the price was far beyond his means so the idea had to be scrapped. But it had taken root in his mind, so he decided to try and make one himself with some of the leather from his shop. On the leather he painstakingly drew the various countries of the world, adding details from time to time, making his lessons glow with the enthusiasm and lively interest of his own heart. The facts that came to light in his endless search enlarged his own world vision, too. Sometimes, his pupils would see their teacher in tears over a geography lesson as he pointed out continents and islands: 'These people are pagans! They have never heard the gospel of saving grace!' he would cry out in deep distress.

It was during this time of testing, when Carey and his wife were so poor they often 'lived for a great while without tasting meat, and with but a scanty pittance of other provision', that the missionary call came into the isolated village. As so often happens, God used an unexpected tool for his purpose.

William was reading *The Last Voyage of Captain Cook*. Ever since his schooldays he had been intensely interested in the travels of the great explorer who was fearless in his effort to discover the hidden lands of the Pacific. Not that Cook himself had any missionary zeal: 'No one would ever venture to introduce Christianity into them, because neither fame nor profit would offer the requisite inducement,' is what he wrote after he made his discoveries. But in this Cook reckoned without William Carey.

As he read of the thrilling voyages Cook had made before his last fatal one in 1779, Carey's mind became obsessed with latitudes and longitudes; with strange people and islands; coral beaches and naked savages; tribal wars and cannibal orgies. As he read, the book became an insistent Macedonian call to Carey. 'Come over and help us!' he could hear them crying.

Hammering on his brain was the thought that these

people needed the gospel of Jesus Christ. He began to study afresh books on church history.

The map on his schoolroom wall began to serve a further purpose. Every nation in the known world was marked on it, with its population, religion, and anything else he could discover. Where he could not afford to buy he found means of borrowing books from others, and day by day the missionary map was extended.

He read the lives of David Brainerd and John Eliot who worked among the Indian people of North America, teaching and translating the Bible into their language. His spirit was stirred afresh, and the Bible came alive with new meaning, seeing in the Old Testament missionary prophecy, and in the New the achievement of missionary adventure.

The map became his prayer-chart, and as he realized the desperate need of the world he became more and more conscious of the riches in Christ that were available, not only to him, but to all who would believe.

He persevered in prayer for the church of his day; that it might once again be revived and lifted out of the listless rut into which it had fallen. He read a pamphlet written by Andrew Fuller: 'It is the duty of those who are entrusted with the Gospel to endeavour to make it known among all nations.' He reread these words again and again as he sat making shoes in his workshop until, at last, he took them to be a direct call from God. In the quietness he answered: 'Here am I, Lord. Send me.' And he meant it.

Carey knew he would first have to arouse the apathetic Christians in the churches, and his first onslaught was made at a ministers' meeting in Northampton.

As the ministers chatted together after the service, old Dr Ryland invited one of the younger men to suggest a subject for discussion. This was Carey's cue and he asked them to consider 'whether the command given to the apostles to teach all nations was not obligatory on all succeeding ministers to the end of the world, seeing that the accompanying promise was of equal extent'.

The proposition was promptly denounced by Dr Ryland.

It has been said that he rebuked Carey with such words as: 'Sit down young man! When God chooses to convert the heathen he will do it without your aid or mine!' But we do not know this for certain.

The harsh words are not easily believed to be those of the established preacher whom Carey had often walked five miles to hear, or to whom the young convert had appealed for instruction in understanding the need and reason for baptism.

It seems obvious that Dr Ryland was greatly moved by the impassioned plea of this enthusiastic pioneer, but he was also concerned that enthusiasm did not hide the enormity of the undertaking. There would be financial difficulties, language barriers and translation problems to face; long and weary voyages to daunt the stoutest heart.

The older man had doubtless come up against more of the unexpected trials of life which he knew William had not yet experienced.

The desire of Dr Ryland was to seek to guide his younger brother in the ministry, and he was desperately anxious for Carey to learn to wait for God's definite timing. Even Andrew Fuller was tempted to think 'If the Lord should make windows in heaven, might such a thing be.'

There were no supporters for Carey and he sat down, disappointed and dejected, but only for a moment. He was not going to allow himself to be discouraged. He knew the depth of human need and his colleagues had yet to catch the vision. However, he was fully determined that they *should* catch it.

The schoolmaster cobbler knew that God had called him and he lost no opportunity of telling others of that call. He talked of it in his preaching; he voiced it in his prayers. At the meetings of ministers he tried to convince his brother ministers of missionary privilege and challenge. One by one he talked to them until the very repetition of the subject left its impression. But still they did not encourage.

This was the hardest tree William had yet tackled, and although the branches continued to elude his grasp, he did not give in.

Studying his map one evening the idea came to turn the facts he had gathered and recorded into a written book. In this way he would be able to reach many more people than would ever be likely to hear his voice.

He called it *An Enquiry into the Obligations of Christians to use Means for the Conversion of the Heathens* and in it he wrote first the facts and details he had collected. Then he stated his arguments, announced his conclusions, and finally put all the fire of his eager missionary heart into the arresting appeal.

He made a rough draft of his book, although he knew that when it was finished he would not have the necessary money to publish.

There were other workers in God's vineyard, however. One day, Carey was visiting Birmingham in connection with the building fund for the new church they needed at Moulton. He called on two gentlemen, one of whom was Mr Thomas Potts who was later to become one of the founders of Birmingham General Hospital.

'Come in and sit down, my friend,' he said kindly to Carey. 'I have wanted to meet you, to hear for myself about your ideas concerning foreign missions. They tell me you talk of little else these days.'

'That is true. I feel it to be of the utmost importance that something should be done for the heathen. It is a burden I cannot shelve,' agreed William, meeting Mr Potts' questioning eyes with a steady gaze.

'But how can this thing be tackled, Mr Carey? And who would be willing to leave this country and go to the heathen?'

The two gentlemen saw his face light up. In his eagerness he stood as he answered.

'My dear friends, I am ready to go wherever God shall call me. I have answered his call and I have told him I am willing to be sent.'

'But where, and how, my friend?' Mr Potts pointed to the chair as he continued. 'Won't you sit down while we talk? You have many miles to walk, and you will be weary before you reach home.'

Carey was thankful to sit down once more, as eagerly he revealed to his listeners the plan that had been forming in his mind for many months.

'If I can find a few friends who will send me out and support me for twelve months, then I am ready to go. God has put before us an open door. Where it will lead

I do not yet know, but no man must seek to close it. If I followed my own desires I would go at once to the islands of the South Seas, starting at Tahiti. If only there were a Society that would send me,' he said with longing.

Although Mr Potts was impressed with the idea, it was so new that he feared it would take time for the Christian public to be prepared for such phenomenal undertakings. He voiced his doubts to William.

'I realize that,' answered Carey. 'They need to know more of the facts. It is for that reason I have gathered them together and am drafting out a booklet on the subject. Were the public to read it I am convinced it would enlighten them concerning their responsibilities.'

'An excellent idea, Carey. When will it be published?' pressed Mr Potts.

'Had I the means to do so I would publish it just as soon as the manuscript is finished.'

Mr Potts smiled: 'Then the public must have the opportunity of considering this important subject! When it is finished we will publish the book, and if necessary I will bear the expense myself. It is obvious you have carefully and clearly considered the whole matter. May God bless you in your labours.'

Carey's foot had touched the highest branch.

Before *Enquiry* was published it was obvious that God was working in the hearts of his people to receive the message it would contain.

The prayer meetings that had been established as a result of the Resolution passed at Nottingham resulted in a wave of spiritual blessing, and the Nonconformist churches in the Midlands were revived. There was a growing desire to spread the gospel throughout the world.

'We pray for these things. Then let us expect them,' they said, encouraging one another when faith began to flag.

5

A Move to Leicester

The work was growing at Moulton. A new building had replaced the small Meeting House when, out of the blue, came an invitation to Carey from Leicester, some thirty miles away. It was a call from Harvey Lane Chapel where a new minister was needed, and in the Autumn of 1789 he took up his new duties there.

Coming as they did from a small country village, life now became something of a bewilderment for the new family transferred into a town with a population of 17,000. A place full of history, and one which had been fortunate in having many benefactors through the years. Men like William Wyggeston, Sir Thomas White and others, whose benefits still surround the city today.

There was a school for boys, endowed by Alderman Gabriel Newton in about 1760. Here pupils were given not only sound academic education, but also instruction in the principles of religion. The infirmary was also established, a well-supported, charitable institution.

By this time there were wide paved streets in Leicester. Brick houses were gradually replacing some of the old timber ones. To Carey's eyes it was an overgrown busy, orderly town, but he rejoiced in the fact that much of the rural aspect still remained. There were many large, old trees and in the spacious market-place stood 'The Pigeon Tree' under which women from the country sat while they sold the pigeons they brought in from the surrounding corn fields. Poultry for the gentlemen's tables!

The old town gates had been finally taken down in 1774, turnpike roads developed, and canals were now bringing cheap coal from Derbyshire.

Like most towns, Leicester had its share of problems with poverty lurking round every corner and workers getting little more than the barest subsistence.

There were riots when a mob broke up new worsted spinning machinery installed by a Mr Whetstone. This act of vandalism was to delay the introduction of worsted spinning machines into Leicester for many years.

This then was the Leicester where Carey and his family now made their home, and where he would earn a living by both cobbling shoes and pastoring the church in Harvey Lane.

For her grocery order Mrs Carey went to the bow-windowed shop in nearby Highcross Street; the stout shoes her husband had made for her tackling the uneven cobblestones with the determination of their maker.

It was not an easy task to be pastor of Harvey Lane at that time for it was a sad church, torn by error. Some members and deacons embraced a fashionable

38

heresy of the age which claimed immunity from obedience to the laws of God on the pretext that if faith alone is sufficient to secure salvation, then a holy life need not necessarily follow.

There were a few members who were seeking to correct this error, and they desperately needed Carey to help them. He realized the difficulties and accepted them as a further challenge. But it took over a year and a whole mountain of grace before the church was restored to a more satisfactory level. By dissolving church membership and readmitting to the new roll only those who were willing to live according to the principles set out in the New Testament, the church began to come alive. Gradually the congregation increased in number and went on growing until it became necessary to add a gallery to the building. Churches in the area felt its influence. People were converted and prayer meetings began to flourish.

The Careys' home was a three-storey cottage opposite the chapel, with small rooms one above the other. On the ground floor was the living-room-cum-workshop, a bedroom above, and on the next floor a room with a small window let into the slope of the roof. This was Carey's study. From the window he could look out at the church he had come to love dearly. But he could see more than that as he visualized the church of Jesus Christ which should stretch across the world. He thought of people in far-off lands who needed Christ. His heart was stirred to pity as he remembered heathen practices that needed the love of Christ to dispel them. There were many nations who could not read the Bible because it was not written in their language.

There was a small garden behind the cottage and

W CAREY
Second by
Shoes bu't
and Sold.

here Carey cultivated flowers and plants which gave him a continual supply of flowers to put in the window of the living-room on the ground floor. It soon became a point of interest to the Leicester citizens as they passed.

'Your window is always full of flowers, Cobbler Carey,' said a woman when she called to pick up her repaired shoes. 'How can you make them grow so plentifully?'

'Perhaps, Madam, it is because I love them. Indeed they are a part of my life. God has given us the seeds and without them we could of course do nothing. But then the good Lord leaves it to us to care for them as they grow.'

During his time in Leicester, Carey met men such as Robert Hall, minister at nearby Arnesby, and Dr Thos Arnold, Robert Brewin and others. He found a great uplift in their friendship and helpfulness. They gave him free access to their libraries and put their literary skill at his disposal. Nothing gave him greater pleasure than talking to these like-minded people of his hopes and longings, discussing with them his problems, and studying the books they lent him. Writing of these years later, to his successor, Carey said: 'It was one of my chief privileges to be favoured with the kind advice, and kinder criticism, of men of the greatest eminence. Their friendship was a jewel I could not too highly prize.'

Also within a few minutes' walk of his cottage there was the ancient Guildhall. This had a unique library which had been open to the public since the previous century. None could have appreciated its wealth of literature and knowledge more than the young

41

preacher who now haunted its doors and poured over the books from its shelves.

But there had to be time for work as well as study. Financially, Carey was slightly better off, but with a wife and three boys now to maintain it was still necessary for him to earn extra from his shoemaking and teaching to add to the salary from the church.

A baby girl was born to them during their time in Leicester, but once again this brought its own sadness for she lived only until her second year.

William worked hard at his cobbling, making sure he was giving his best service to his customers. When this was finished for the day he made time to study languages, science, history; to lecture when invited, and weekly to preach. It was a busy life but a contented one. In a letter to his father written at this time he said: 'I am not my own, nor would I choose for myself. Let God employ me where he thinks fit.'

All the problems and difficulties could not draw Carey's mind away from his central theme—world evangelism. He talked of it to his brother ministers, stressing the urgent need for it. Gradually they were coming to see the truth of this need but they lacked the courage to go forward and attempt to do anything about it. What could a few poor pastors accomplish? 'It may come later maybe, but the time is not yet,' they said to each other.

It was Easter. The time of year when new life appears in the bare places of the earth and she rejoices in resurrection. On April 27th, 1791 the ministers from Leicestershire, and adjoining Northamptonshire, met for a meeting at Clipstone, where the speakers were to be Andrew Fuller and John Sutcliff.

Carey worked late the night before, then closed his shop, and left his cobbling for the day, to attend the meeting. The words of the preachers rejoiced his heart as they reminded their congregation of the danger of delay when doing the Lord's work.

Fuller spoke from Haggai 1:2, and warned: 'It becomes us to beware lest we account that impossible which only requires such a degree of exertion as we are not inclined to give. We pray for the conversion of the world and yet we neglect the ordinary means by which it can be brought about.... How shall they hear without a preacher?'

To Carey's disappointment the other ministers present were not sufficiently moved to take immediate action. They would not yet form a Missionary Society in spite of the urgent need for one, the details of which he had spelt out so clearly in *Enquiry*. It was possibly with an idea of gaining time, and at the same time consoling their enthusiastic colleague, that finally they suggested he revise the book before he sought to get it published.

He returned to his attic study to review his manuscript. He could see that with the opportunities he now had for wider reading there were certain alterations he could make and there were new truths to add. This he did, with his usual forthright determination. When the book was published within the year no reader missed the convincing missionary appeal.

Enquiry contained five chapters on practical Christian obligation, the needs of the world, the opportunities, and proposals for the formation of a Society. Obedience and obligation were the two words that set the theme, and the whole work throbbed with the heartbeats of its author. It was a masterpiece.

Years later Dr George Smith wrote: 'The Enquiry has a literary interest of its own, as a contribution to the statistics and geography of the world, written in a cultured and almost finished style such as few, if any, university men of that day could have produced, for none were impelled by such a motive as Carey had.'

6

The Birth of the Missionary Society

Once people had been given the opportunity to read
Enquiry the author proceeded to press home the message it contained.

It was just a year since the meeting at Clipstone,
and the next Association meeting was to be held in the
Baptist Chapel in Park Street, Nottingham. William
Carey had been asked to preach.

In the quiet of his study he prayed over his sermon
as he prepared it. He sought earnestly for the right
words to move the heart of a congregation made up
mostly of fellow ministers. These were the people he
longed to reach and to convince. The longings,
thoughts and prayers of years built up his address,
paragraph by paragraph.

At last the day arrived. It was in the month of May
and Nottingham was a busy place, caught up in its
trading, buying and selling, unaware of the young
cobbler who was coming to be the speaker in the
Baptist Chapel. Few, if any of them, knew he was also
the pastor of Harvey Lane Chapel in Leicester, twenty-

five miles away.

There were ministers and others who had gathered in Nottingham from as far away as Northampton and district. Their horses clattered up to the courtyard of 'The Angel', a large inn in the wide market-place where they were to put up for the night.

Honest country farmers arrived on horseback, alone, or in some cases they drove the vehicle carrying wife and family. Pedestrians, dusty and travel-stained, mingled with the black-coated ministers, thankful to be at the end of many weary miles.

They talked of the recent anti-slavery debate in the Commons and of its defeat; of Wilberforce, the powerful Parliamentarian, and his speeches in the House. There were murmurs about the East India Company, and worried conversation about troubles in France.

Then their talk inevitably turned to the matter in hand and their reason for being present. They spoke of the enthusiastic young man who was to be the speaker at the conference, the minister who had been stirring up the lethargic churches to try and make them hear the call of lands less favoured than their own. This was the man who talked incessantly of the needs of nations who had not yet heard the gospel of Jesus Christ. They were eager to listen to his preaching.

The Baptist Chapel was a simple building beside the almshouses. Early on the morning of May 31st the congregation gathered to pray. Then at 10 o'clock they returned to sit on hard benches, curious to hear what the slight young man with the ill-fitting wig would have to say to them.

When he announced his text there was a hint of surprise among the listeners.

'Enlarge the place of thy tent...spare not, lengthen thy cords, and strengthen thy stakes.' It was found in Isaiah 54:2.

Most of them knew it. Some of the ministers had doubtless used the verse in their own sermons, but they had not seen it in the light of a missionary command. They listened critically as Carey introduced his subject and then lifted it to the very gates of heaven with words that still echo down the years.

'Expect great things *from* God. Attempt great things *for* God.'

Into his sermon he poured all the longings of his heart for the past eight years. Over and over he repeated the phrase until it sank into the hearts of those who heard. The words came from the soul of the preacher and spread across his listeners with the impact of an explosion. They were jolted out of their lethargy as the Holy Spirit moved among them. It was the era of long and ponderous sermons, but this time the address was short and simple. This was a burning bush of missionary enterprise, calling to the listless churches of the day to enlarge their tents, to lengthen their self-centred cords, to widen their vision.

Carey told them: 'God is calling you to a brilliant future, to preach the gospel throughout the world. My friends, you need this wider vision.'

In the shade of Nottingham's famous castle he reminded his hearers of the great commission given on the Galilean hillside. 'Go ye.' It meant what it said, he emphasized, and his earnest sincerity stirred the conscience of everyone present.

When he finished speaking he sat down. There was silence, then began a buzz of talk among the people. The preacher was a man with something to say, certainly, and it was obvious he knew his subject well. He had roused their interest and they must find out more. Like a magnet they were drawn to the bookstall, eager to buy a copy of his book, to read *Enquiry* for themselves.

But for Carey there was to be yet another disappointment as he discovered how quickly people's enthusiasm can fall from the heady heights of the mountain top down into the sonorous less demanding, shades of the valley.

To his dismay, he found that when the ministers

met next morning for their conference the fire had died out of their eagerness. The Tempter had been busy reminding them of the tremendous difficulties in the path suggested, overpowering them with cold, calculating reason.

Once more they were asking themselves: 'What can a mere handful of preachers accomplish?' It was true they had been inspired by Carey's sermon yesterday, and his proposals were good enough. For the time being, however, they were not practical.

But this time Carey was adamant. He refused to allow the matter to be completely put aside and forgotten. He pleaded with them. In great distress he begged his brother ministers not to separate before a definite plan was formed. They still doubted, but by sheer perseverance he so far overcame their doubts as to win from them a decision to pass a resolution for a plan to be prepared for forming a society to send the gospel to other countries.

It remained a source of deep disappointment to Carey that his colleagues had not responded more eagerly to the message which he was convinced God had given him to pass on to them. His patience was sorely tried, his enthusiasm sadly dampened, but he determined not to be in despair. This was a tree he had set himself to climb and though it was proving to be the most difficult one he had yet tackled, he would come back to it again and again until he had gained the highest branch.

Deep in his heart he was sure that a Missionary Society would eventually be formed, and his next step must be the preparation of the proposed plan.

Carefully he set to work, writing down every detail

of the plan, and before the next meeting of the association in the following October, he had it ready to put before them.

With the plan under his arm he scarcely noticed the miles he had to walk to get to Kettering for the meeting. He was filled with a great joy at the nearness of the goal for which he had been striving, for surely the church could no longer delay.

It was not until after the public meeting that the plan was discussed. A small group of twelve ministers, one student and one layman met in the home of a widow, Mrs Wallis. Carefully Carey opened out the precious document and he laid it on the table before them. They were determined to stifle the doubts that were still threatening to rise in their hearts to remind them of the many obstacles to be overcome. They knew the project would cost more money than they could envisage; they were pitifully few in number, but at last they had caught the vision. Carey's faith and enthusiasm were contagious, and now they shared his longing to make Christ known to all the world.

After so much tribulation and travail they could hear the first faint cries of the groping infant, and before they dispersed that evening the Missionary Society was born.

First they drew up a resolution: 'Humbly desirous of making an effort for the propagation of the Gospel amongst the heathen, according to the recommendations of Carey's "Enquiry", we unanimously resolve to act in society together for this purpose; and as in the divided state of Christendom each denomination, by exerting itself separately, seems likeliest to accomplish the great end, we name this: "The Particular Baptist

Society for the Propagation of the Gospel amongst the Heathen."'

The fourteen people present drew up a subscription list. It was unlikely any of them had much money with them, so it was suggested that they wrote on slips of paper the amount they felt they could afford as an annual subscription. They agreed that half a guinea should be the minimum for each membership. Then their written promises were gathered together, and the slips of paper were dropped into Andrew Fuller's snuff box, which lay conveniently to hand. An annual income of £13.2.6d was promised. Some of the subscriptions were handed in at the next meeting of the society a month later, but several members needed longer to save the amount out of their meagre wages.

But on that evening of October 2nd, 1792 there were fourteen triumphant Christians who might well have been reminded of the hymn that Isaac Watts had written earlier in their century: 'Jesus shall reign where'er the sun does his successive journeys run.'

It was a jubilant Carey who returned home to Leicester, conscious that he was no longer working alone. Others were now committed to the great venture of evangelizing and were pledged to give their money, time and, if need be, their life.

Before the first meeting of the society, the following month, new subscribers had been added to the list. A donation of twenty pounds came from someone as far away as Northumberland. Samuel Pearce had inspired his people at Birmingham with the thrill of missionary giving and they contributed seventy pounds.

'Faith is the substance of things hoped for, the evidence of things not seen' (Heb 11:1).

51

7

'I Will Go To India'

The committee met again to discuss details. Where would the best openings for missionary work be found? What qualifications were required in a missionary? Who would be willing to go? There were so many questions waiting to be answered.

Carey was unable to attend this meeting, but he sent the committee a letter he had received from a Dr Thomas, who had been working for several years as a medical missionary in Bengal. He was now in England where he was seeking to establish a fund for a mission to be started in Bengal, and to find a companion to help him there. He had heard of the newly-formed Missionary Society and he was eager to contact its members.

For a long time Carey had been concerned over the desperate needs of India, and this had superseded his first idea of offering to go to Tahiti. God had tied strings round his missionary heart which were drawing him ever nearer to the people of that vast land.

He suggested that the secretary of the society,

Andrew Fuller, should write to Thomas and ask for details of himself, his work and his views on missionary work in Bengal. The reply from Thomas satisfied the committee that here was a Christian man, fearless in his confession of Christ as Lord, and the details of his work among the Hindus indicated his zeal as a missionary. It was felt that they had found someone worthy of support.

The letter from Thomas did not tell of his kind but restless heart; of his courageous spirit that seemed to court almost unnecessary danger, or his somewhat careless attitude to responsibility. Nor did it tell of his vital temperament made up of the reds and scarlets of life; of his great love for the down-trodden heathen and his willingness to spend and be spent in service to them. There was no mention of his lack of business acumen, and the unfortunate positions in which he was so often placed as a result. Nor did it mention his many blunders, or his careless approach to the financial side of life; his aptitude to annoy people unwittingly, and the charm which was so much a part of him that they invariably forgave him!

These things only came to light later as circumstances eventually revealed them. But through it all one could discern in Dr Thomas the fire of a great love for his Saviour, and a heart set on winning the people of India to him.

It was arranged for Thomas to meet the committee at Kettering on January 10th, 1793. When he and Carey saw each other they were instantly united in one absorbing desire, and they met as friends. Questions about India came thick and fast from the committee. What were the expenses likely to be? What was life in

India like, and how did it compare with 18th-century England?

Thomas told of India's great need, its poverty, its cruel heathen practices, and its readiness to listen to a story of redeeming love. Carey listened with rapt attention to it all, and he felt a tearing in his heart for these people. He must go to India and tell the story of Jesus Christ.

The last barrier was broken down when he heard Thomas say that a missionary could be self-supporting in India after the first few months of arriving there. Carey had insisted in his *Enquiry* that a pioneer should only need assistance for the initial outlay on the mission field. Now this was being confirmed by one who had experienced it.

'I will go to India,' he exclaimed. 'I will go, but you at home must hold the ropes.'

But Thomas, in his keenness to get back to the India he loved, was covering many of the real facts. He may not have realized he was being misleading, nor that he was painting the picture with colours of a spectrum all his own.

Even if he had been told of the many difficulties and expenses that would have to be met, Carey would still have been willing to go. But his grasp on this particularly high bough of the tree needed to be firm as he walked thoughtfully home after the meeting. It had been suggested that he and Thomas sail in the coming Spring. How would Dorothy, his timid, retiring wife, react to this piece of startling news? He hardly dared think.

Dorothy was a country girl who had never travelled more than thirty miles from the place where she was born and brought up. Until she came to live at Leicester she had hardly been outside her own village. Could her love for William prove strong enough to contemplate a voyage filled with dangers; to live in a strange land of frightening, unknown ways?

What about their three sons? They would have to be considered. The fact that another baby was due in a few months also had to be faced.

As he trudged along the lonely country lanes William was troubled, in spite of his jubilation. It was not for himself but for his wife and family. The prospect was a fearful one for a pioneer in those days of distance, uncertainty and ignorance. There were none of the globe-shrinking facilities of our modern age to offer help to them. Very little was known of India and her way of life, and it was fifteen thousand danger-ridden miles away.

Carey thought about how, since their marriage, he had taught Dorothy to read. The task had needed all the patience he could muster for she did not find learning an easy task. Could she now be willing to go and live among people who could not even speak to her in that same language? He reflected that it was he who had built the altar and for himself there was no thought of turning away, but how right was it to ask his wife to share in the sacrifice? To go without her would mean death to his happiness, but if that were the only alternative, then so be it.

It was nearly morning when William reached home, cold as stone, desperately hungry and thirsty. Very soon Dorothy had the kettle boiling on the hob. As they sat drinking their hot tea Carey told his wife of his plans.

'Go to India?' she gasped. 'No, William, never!'

She looked at him with bewildered eyes. Leave their little home and everyone they knew? It was un- thinkable.

'We cannot go, William! We have our children to think of. There is your church here, and your home. Surely God wouldn't want you to leave everything?'

'My dear, you don't understand. I know God has asked me to go to India for him. He has called me. I have answered and I cannot draw back. I would not if I could,' replied William, urgently, willing her to understand.

But Dorothy was adamant. Fuller and Sutcliff heard that she refused to go to India so they travelled to Leicester to try to persuade her to change her mind. It was of no use and she declared that if William must go, then she would remain here with her children and prepare herself for the parting.

Carey was grieved beyond telling and but for his firm faith and devotion to Christ he might even yet have given up the project. However, during the following week he wrote to his father at Paulerspury: '...I hope, dear father, you may be enabled to sur- render me up to the Lord for the most arduous, honourable, and important work that ever any of the sons of men were called to engage in. I have many sacrifices to make. I must part with a beloved family and a number of most affectionate friends.... But I have set my hand to the plough.'

'Is William mad?' shouted his father when he read the letter.

The following Sunday William broke the news to his large congregation at Harvey Lane. At first they were dumb with grief at the thought of losing such a pastor whose faithful ministry had been a source of such blessing. Some even refused to give him up, maintaining that it was not right for him to leave a work when God was using his ministry so remarkably.

But gradually they came to see that this was in fact God answering their prayer for the spread of Christ's kingdom among the heathen, and that he was asking them to join in the first sacrifice. When they realized this they were not only prepared to let him go, but were ready to back him in every way possible, rejoicing in the fact that they were the church that was sending him. Even so, they wrote in the church minute book: 'Though it is at the expense of losing one whom we love as our own souls.'

In the end it was arranged that Carey should take his eldest son, Felix, with him to India, and return in a year or two for his wife and the other children.

No other cause would have made him give up his family and he did not falter. Only if God himself provided a 'ram in the thicket', as he did for Abraham, could there be any deviation in the sacrifice.

8

Farewell England For Ever

Now it was time to put personal problems aside and turn to the practical matter of finance for the project. It was difficult to determine exactly how much the fares would cost for Carey and his son, and Dr Thomas and his wife. There were no fixed rates to guide an intending voyager.

They would need to take with them sufficient money to live on while the work was in the early stages in India, and also leave provision for the family left in England.

There were just four months in which to raise the required amount which would be at least £550. This was a staggering sum for a struggling shoemaker to think about, and by this time he had learnt that Thomas could contribute nothing but debts!

Expect great things from God. Carey had said it so many times in his memorable sermon in Nottingham, and many more times since then in his heart. Now it ran along the corridors of his mind, encouraging, assuring, reminding him of the greatness of the God he was anxious to serve. He refused to be dismayed.

He and his faithful band of helpers sent out letters, making the project and its needs known to Baptists in other parts of the country. The response was small, for many were afraid to commit themselves to supporting so wild a venture. Such was the thinking at that time that some ministers would not even mention the idea of the gospel being preached to the heathen. 'The time is not yet,' they repeated to one another, shaking their heads over this too enthusiastic young man.

Carey, Thomas and Fuller toured the country for three months seeking to rouse Christians from their sleep of indifference. They pleaded for prayer backing, vital for the success of the mission. Gradually the great things they were expecting began to happen, with first just a sprinkling of small amounts of money which grew bigger as people began to realize their responsibilities. The money was coming in, but even more important was the interest in the mission which was becoming evident.

In the city of Bath Thomas spoke to a crowded meeting, explaining the need for missionaries, seeking interest and prayer from the people at home, and asking for generous giving to enable the work to be started.

His appeal in this instance appeared to fall on deaf ears, and the resultant contribution was one penny. But Thomas understood people, even if they didn't always understand him! He got up to thank the meeting for their interest, casually mentioning the fact that all results were being recorded in the Mission book. He would enter theirs. 'Bath: one penny.' As he expected, they were embarrassed into action and the final result was a gift of twenty-two pounds!

Samual Pearce talked to his people in Birmingham, who were already interested in missionary giving. He suggested they form a local auxiliary to the Missionary Society and when this was done it was hoped other towns would follow suit.

Now came the exciting problem of arranging their passage to India. The only English vessels sailing there were controlled by the East India Company who were antagonistic towards missionary work. A few years previously an Act of Parliament had made it illegal for anyone to live in the British possessions of India without a licence from the Company. What hope was there of securing this licence? Could the missionaries reach India without it? They deliberated. They prayed. Then they decided to try.

Thomas knew the captain of the East Indian *Earl of Oxford,* a ship on which he had once acted as surgeon, and this was now in England preparing for its next voyage. Captain White agreed to take them to Calcutta without a permit, and final arrangements were made to leave England in the middle of April.

Their little home was once again packed into wooden boxes and transported on a farmer's wagon back to Dorothy's native Piddington. They had been able to secure a cottage there and Dorothy's younger sister, Katherine, had arranged to live with her and help look after the family.

When they arrived, tired and miserable from the uncomfortable journey, sad because of the coming parting, Katherine welcomed them with a cheerful smile. Carey blessed her in his heart for it lifted a fragment of the burden, knowing that his wife would be among her own people, and be loved and cared for.

During the meal that Katherine had prepared for them his thoughts turned to the many plans accumulating in his mind. He would seek to help the people of India and minister to their spiritual needs. While Thomas used his medical skill for the healing of their bodies, he himself must learn quickly to read Bengali. The gift God had given him for mastering languages could be used to translate the Scriptures into the native tongue. Eventually they would open schools.

He thought of that young man he met recently, William Ward, an earnest Christian who had mentioned the fact that he was a printer by trade. He was so interested in the proposed mission that Carey had talked of the plans he had in mind. When they parted he said to Ward: 'I hope, with God's blessing, to have the Bible translated and ready for the press in four or five years. You must come out and print it for us!'

It was in actual fact seven years before the translation was ready, but by that time Ward was with Carey in Bengal.

The days at Piddington went by quickly. All too soon for Dorothy the farewells had to be made. She was sick at heart, not only dreading the long separation in front of them, but knowing that this was something she had herself imposed.

They embarked on the *Earl of Oxford* on April 4th, 1793 with a strange mixture of exhilaration and sadness. The vessel sailed from the Thames as far as Ryde, Isle of Wight, to await a convoy, without which no passenger-ship would dare to leave. As the days stretched into weeks, Carey and his party decided to take rooms in Ryde until the ship sailed for India.

This delay was frustrating, but it proved useful to Thomas's creditors who heard that he was leaving the country and sent for him to first come back and settle outstanding debts. Alarmed and shocked, Carey could only wait to find out what the consequences of this state of affairs would mean to the mission. Subsequent events lost no time in supplying the answer.

While Thomas was away the captain of the *Earl of Oxford* developed 'cold feet' about his offer to take the missionaries without the East India Company's leave. The risk suddenly appeared too great. He would take Mrs Thomas and her daughter but finally refused to take the others.

Moved almost to tears as he watched the ship disappearing over the skyline, Carey's heart was in a tumult. What was God doing to him? Was this to be the ignominious end of all his hopes to reach India? He was indeed downcast, but not in complete despair. God was moving in mysterious ways but his wonders would be, must be, brought to pass. His servants must go on expecting the great things that had been promised.

Carey and Felix returned to Portsmouth and took the coach to London. There was news from home that the expected baby had arrived and he now had another son. He had written to his wife: 'If I had all the world I would freely give it all to have you and the children with me.' With this unexpected change of plan there might be an opportunity to see them all once more.

They linked up with Thomas in London. He was deeply remorseful, but still buoyant enough to make furtive enquiries in a coffee-house to find out if there was any ship, not under the control of the Company, that might be sailing to India.

They heard that a Danish boat, the *Kron Princessa Maria*, was on her way from Copenhagen and expected shortly. They learnt that the fare for the three of them would be £250. All they had was the sum refunded by the captain of the *Earl of Oxford*, £150, but in faith they booked their passage.

Then, like a couple of excited schoolboys suddenly released from lessons, they dashed off to Piddington to see the family again before the Danish ship would be ready to sail.

Although it was early morning when Carey and his friend reached the village, many of the cottagers saw them and came running out to greet the unexpected visitors who they thought would by this time be far away on the high seas.

When William lifted the latch of the cottage door and walked in, it was no wonder Dorothy looked, gasped, and burst into tears. She was dreaming. She must be. A dream that was too good to be true! Then surprise gave place to delight and eagerly she fetched the new baby to meet his father.

As her sister Katherine prepared a hurried breakfast for them all, Carey took the opportunity to appeal to his wife once more to change her mind and go with him to India. They prayed together over the matter but still Dorothy was too afraid to take what seemed to be such a dangerous step into the dark.

When the time came to say goodbye the two men and Felix set out to walk to Northampton in the hope of seeing Dr Ryland and getting help to raise the additional money needed for the passage. Carey was so overcome with grief at the parting that after a few miles Thomas, whose sympathetic nature could not bear to see it, decided they must return and make one more effort.

Dorothy's loving heart could stand no more, and in tears she said she would go if her sister would go too. Taken aback by this sudden turn of events, Katherine had only a few minutes to make up her mind. She sent up a quick prayer for guidance.

'I am ready to go with you if that is what you want,' she said.

Now the cottage came alive with activity as the two women sorted and packed essentials for themselves, and the four children, ready for their journey to the other side of the world. Just twenty-four hours later they were ready to start out!

When they reached Dover, Thomas the Pleader persuaded the captain's agent to take the complete family on special terms, he and Katherine being willing to travel as 'attendants'. So by this means the sum of 300 guineas which they had managed to accumulate was sufficient.

Early in the morning of June 13th, 1793, the whole family went aboard the sailing ship *Kron Princessa Maria* and all hundred and thirty feet of her length seemed to Carey as pure gold. This was the ship that was to take not only himself, but his wife and children, across the vast ocean to an unknown land. He was at last on his way to a people he already loved because of their need, and to a work that was dearer to him than life itself.

The England that had given him birth, and taught him much of life and its meaning, became smaller as he and Dorothy stood on deck and watched its coastline grow blurred, before passing for ever from their view. They never returned to this country.

Life on the ship was a strange, bewildering experience for the family, but the extreme kindness of the captain made up for many of the discomforts. He was an Englishman who had become a naturalized Danish subject and he was greatly impressed when he learned the purpose of Carey's journey.

The family were accommodated in the main cabin: 'Half the width of the ship, with south windows and papered sides.' There was a smaller cabin given for Katherine and another for Thomas, and the captain insisted that the whole party should take meals at his table.

There was a novelty about it all to start with, but this wore off as day after day the ship ploughed through the waters, with nothing to look at but surrounding sea. The dreaded Bay of Biscay lived up to its reputation and the voyagers suffered the miseries of sea sickness. It was little wonder that, in the words of Thomas, 'Mrs Carey had many fears and troubles, so that she was like Lot's wife until we passed the Cape.'

It was all of five months after leaving England before the hazardous voyage came to an end. Storms had battered and tossed the ship, sun in the tropics scorched and becalmed her, violent currents had tantalized and kept her for a whole month within two hundred miles of Bengal.

William spent much time on the voyage in study of the Bengali language, helped by Thomas. In return, Carey used his knowledge of Hebrew to assist his colleague in completing a translation of the book of Genesis.

Many of his friends back in England would have had difficulty in recognizing Carey as he stepped off the boat on to Indian soil. Illness and anxiety in his early life had caused premature baldness, and for several years he had worn an ill-fitting wig. Ryland had referred to it as 'odious' and said of the man who made it: 'Good Mr Wilson of Olney is an excellent Christian, but one of the ugliest wigmakers that ever was born...enough to spoil any man's physiognomy!'

It may be that Carey himself began to realize this during the long and wearisome voyage, for one day he took off the wig and threw it overboard.

His decision to take this drastic action could have been due to the heat of the tropics, or maybe his wife took advantage of her captive audience! It could have been the result of a quiet word from her, claiming the discarding of the ugly wig as her reward for being willing at last to go with her husband to India!

9

In Calcutta

Carey felt a deep sense of urgency as they landed at Calcutta in November. He must proceed with what he knew to be his life work. India was already like a much loved child to him. He knew its shape, its size and its population. He had made notes of the religions of its people and he knew of its turmoil and war.

Portugal had lost power but still held some of the Indian ports. Dutch rule had almost disappeared, and the Danish East India Company had only a small territory around Tranquebar in the south, and at Serampore on the river Hooghly, sixteen miles to the north of Calcutta. England was in power in the south and Bengal was in the hands of the British East India Company. This was slowly developing into a governing power, with its own territories and armies, administrators and princes.

Among the Europeans in India the moral tone was low. They were mostly servants of the East India Company, and they excused their lax morals on the grounds of separation from home and the general disadvantages of life in a tropical country.

There had been one or two brave attempts to spread the gospel by solitary individuals, or small communities, from time to time. The Danish-Hallé Mission, organized by King Frederick IV of Denmark, also had workers there.

Several years previously a Mr Charles Grant, who held a high position with the East India Company, had been concerned about the need for missionary work among the Indian people. When the Rev. David Brown arrived as chaplain to a military orphanage in Calcutta in 1786, he found a kindred spirit in Mr Grant. They discussed the idea of a mission to the people of Bengal with John Thomas. Mr Grant was able to approach influential people to secure their interest in the scheme, and he wrote to the Archbishop of Canterbury, John Newton, William Wilberforce, and the Countess of Huntingdon, among others. He also gained from the Governor General a promise not to oppose the scheme.

At first Grant had employed Thomas to do missionary work among the employees at his factory at Gumalti, but soon there was friction. The two men were temperamentally opposed and their views on religious doctrine differed. Thomas's fiery, impulsive nature would not bend to the kind, but firm, remonstrances of the more serene Grant. It was then that the two had parted company, Thomas to return to England to seek fresh support and find someone to help him in the work of evangelizing. This was when he had linked up with Carey and the English Baptists.

This did not affect the zeal of Grant or his interest in the work.

The charter of the East India Company had to go up before Parliament for renewal every twenty years, and the time was due. Grant persuaded Wilberforce to include in the charter a clause to recognize the need for moral improvement of the people of India and the duty of promoting its religious life. The resolutions he laid before Parliament sought to legalize the preaching and spreading of the gospel.

On May 14th the House passed the clauses which referred to the sending out of ministers of religion and chaplains to minister to the Europeans, and also one which empowered the East India Company to send schoolmasters and others for the religious and moral improvement of the people. But the Court of Directors were alarmed at such a resolution and violently opposed it, stating that the conversion of the nationals would be a disaster.

When it came up for the third reading, the House threw out the proposals. So the old charter was renewed for the next twenty years and the Company set themselves out to prevent missionary work in all Indian territories under their control.

This was the state of affairs when Carey and Thomas landed as the first two Englishmen to be sent by a Missionary Society to work as missionaries to the Indian people.

10

Early Days

The party had arrived in Calcutta, and landed without permits and without the knowledge of the authorities. They were indeed aliens in a foreign country, in a town with a population of about 200,000 people made up of Europeans and Indians. A town with only one carriage road, the dusty 'Course'.

It was a relief to them all that Thomas knew Calcutta, and they looked to him to take the best steps possible to establish them suitably in this strange place of contrasting fine houses, and squalid native quarters.

They stayed in Calcutta long enough to effect the sale of the goods they brought out with them for this purpose, and this meant they had £150 in ready money. Then they moved to Bendel, a Portuguese settlement about three miles away, where they hoped to be able to live economically. They found a small house to rent, and bought a boat to reach the villages along the river so that they could preach to the people.

It was not long before it became obvious to Carey

that their money would not last long without further income, and he began to look for some means of augmenting it. Hearing that the Company needed a botanist to look after their Botanical Gardens in Calcutta, he returned there to apply for the position. He found the vacancy had been filled.

A kindly Indian took pity on this now homeless family and allowed them to live temporarily in his garden-house at Manicktulla, a suburb of Calcutta. Meanwhile, Thomas set up as a surgeon in the town to quieten his ever persistent creditors.

Carey knew he would not be able to stay permanently in Calcutta as a missionary even had he been able to afford to do so. The climate, the unaccustomed food and the tropical life, coming after the strain of the long voyage, did nothing to help his family to settle. Dorothy and the two older boys were ill with dysentery and this added to their inevitable homesickness.

Everything was conspiring to make Carey feel dejected and alone, harassed and perplexed. To his dismay he learnt from Thomas that the whole year's allowance had been spent, although they had been in India for less than ten weeks. This was alarming for they could not hope for more money to be sent out till the following Autumn.

It seemed that the city of sunshine had nothing to offer but gloom and despondency. As Carey reviewed his life during these days of trial it looked as if circumstances had indeed torn it into worthless fragments. As yet he was not able to see these shreds through God's kaleidoscope where every piece fitted to make a perfect pattern. A movement of the hand holding the instrument was sufficient to change the pattern but this did not mar it or dull its beauty. Gradually he came to realize this and even as he brooded, something of the peace of God came through to him.

On January 17th he wrote in his diary: 'Towards evening felt the all-sufficiency of God and the stability of His promises . . . I was able to roll my cares on Him.' Later he wrote: 'Everything is known to God and He cares for the Mission. I rejoice in having undertaken this work and I shall, even if I lose my life.'

When he was offered a piece of land at Debhatta in the Sunderbans, with the possibility of being able to use the bungalow belonging to the Salt Department, he accepted it, together with the cobras and tigers he knew lived in the forests round about. He claimed the promise of God for protection from these dangers.

He took with him the pundit he had engaged, Ram Ram Basu, who could speak English and would be able to act as interpreter, and they set off on the journey of three days by boat through the Salt Lakes.

When they arrived they were in for another disappointment for they found the bungalow was already occupied, but Mr Charles Short, the Company's assistant, invited the whole family to his own home. He was the kindest of men but had no time for missionary work, considering the whole project an absurdity. In taking in these strangers he was unaware of how much he was helping their cause, but his kind heart gave them welcome as his guests for all the months of their need. He insisted on supplying whatever they needed.

It was not surprising that Katherine fell in love with this big-hearted bachelor, and when later he asked her to marry him she consented happily.

Carey liked Debhatta. It was a chief village on the

East bank of the River Jubuna. His ailing family were slowly recovering, and it was a great relief to be so comfortably housed in the home of Mr Short. But it was necessary to make plans for a permanent home. He chose a piece of land to cultivate, and a site on which to build a house. With little more than a spade by way of tools he worked hard to make a clearing in the jungle, and then began on the little house of bamboo, grass mats and thatch. He fenced in a patch of ground to make a garden and here he planted vegetables.

The nationals, encouraged by having an Englishman with a gun living there, began to return to the district they had forsaken through fear of tigers. Carey could visualize a colony growing up around him who looked to him as their protector, and to whom he would certainly hope to become a pastor.

He was intensely interested in everything he discovered in this new land of his adoption. He saw rare birds, strange insects and plants, and he added exciting specimens to the collection he had begun as a small boy in an English village. The open-air life suited him, and gradually the health of the whole family improved.

He took with him his pundit when he went to preach to the people in the villages on both sides of the Jubuna. They accepted him and were ready to listen to what he had to say with wide-eyed interest. 'Preachers are needed a thousand times more than people to preach to,' he wrote. He was greatly encouraged when on one occasion a group of Brahmins came up to him where he was working, and openly thanked him for coming to live among them.

But there was much to sadden him as well. He was

73

deeply distressed when he saw people practising self-torture such as hook-swinging. For this horrific ceremony hooks are fastened into the flesh on either side of a man's back. Strings attached to the hooks are tied to a rope at one end of a horizontal bamboo. The other end of the rope is held by several men who, by their running, turn the whole contraption round in circles. The tortuously suspended devotee scatters herbs offered to Siva, a Hindu god, and will swing for something like a quarter of an hour.

While these things nauseated and shocked Carey they also increased his longing to learn the language of the people so that he could more effectively talk to them of a Saviour's love.

He was carrying out what seemed to be a very worthwhile task at Debhatta, but there was an even greater one on the horizon for him. He received a letter from Thomas at Malda telling Carey that he had secured for himself an important position as manager of an indigo 'out-work' that was being planted.

This was good news indeed but there was more to follow. The letter went on to say that another similar position had become vacant at Mudnabatty and Thomas had suggested to his employer, Mr Udney, that Carey might be considered for this.

It was a shaking of the kaleidoscope that the missionary had not anticipated, but he felt it could be God's opening door for him. The salary offered was a generous one, and would enable him to allocate a large amount towards the cost of the publication of the Scriptures. It would also be good to have Christian fellowship and friendship, and Mr Udney assured him that he would have time for missionary work and study apart from his duties. This was most important to Carey, for above all else he wanted to continue his translation work.

By May 23rd, 1794 everything was settled. Carey said goodbye to Mr Short after thanking him with a grateful heart for all his kindness. When the family set off they were one less in number, for Katherine stayed behind to marry their kindly benefactor!

They looked forward to the boat trip of 300 miles with mixed feelings. It would mean three weeks in the fierce glare of the tropical sun with temperatures around 110 degrees, the only shade they had was provided by a straw canopy. The discomfort was aggravated by the unwelcome attention of the mosquitoes, quick to relish the taste of English blood! No wonder Carey wrote in his journal: 'In the afternoon I felt peevish and uncomfortable.'

In spite of all this there was an exciting fascination about the sights and sounds around them as they floated down the river. There were barges passing by constantly and these were loaded with goods of all descriptions, the noisy crews calling to other boats as they passed.

There were unusual trees and fruits growing on the banks of the water. Bright crimson-spotted 'Flamboyant' or flame trees lit up their surroundings like a flame of fire. Further away on the hills were the high Indian laburnums, and the fragrance of the flowers came to them on the evening breeze. They caught fleeting glimpses of the villages with their busy markets, the noise of them subdued by distance.

Exotic birds flew overhead, rising startled from the foliage of the banks as the boat approached. On the mud banks were always the sleepy, slippery crocodiles. Sometimes, in the evening, they would hear the haunting sound of the sittar instrument, its eerie melody mingling with the cries of the wildlife disturbed in the darkness of the vast Indian night.

Although Carey found great pleasure in discovering all the new wonders around him, he also learned that living on a boat with four boisterous sons, and a delicate wife didn't provide ideal conditions for language and Bible study.

Dorothy was missing the comfort of her sister, Katherine, and her help with the care of the children, and William needed to become general assistant and nursemaid! He resigned himself to the situation, saying it was all part of being a missionary. 'Travelling with a family is a great hindrance to holy, spiritual meditation,' he confided to his journal, but whenever an opportunity did present itself he would snatch a few moments of quiet and persevere with his studies.

On June 15th, 1794, a hot sticky day, the boat tied up at Malda on the Maharunda River accompanied by much bumping, scraping and the usual noisy shouting and fluster.

With relief the family stepped ashore. They were welcomed into the comfortable home of Mr Udney before finally settling into their new house, which was waiting for them. Here they were able to relax, thankful to be back on terra firma once more, and when Sunday came Carey was asked to preach to the Europeans in the district. As he rose to speak who should he see in the congregation but his old friend Dr Thomas. Mr Udney had invited him to join them for the day. After the service the two friends eagerly chatted and exchanged news. There was much to tell each other.

II

Indigo-Making

Now Carey was to learn a new industry. To give him first-hand knowledge of the process, Mr Udney arranged for him to visit the best indigo concerns in the area.

The land round Mudnabatty was flat, open country watered by the Ganges, with rice fields stretching out as far as the eye could see. Little villages were dotted about, surrounded by mango and banyan trees. Here and there were clusters of bamboo or perhaps, a solitary palm.

The prickly-pear was there in abundance and provided an ideal hiding place for the snakes which were not as easily avoided as the crocodiles that lay in the rivers and pools.

In spite of the hazards there was a quiet restfulness about the pace with its gently waving green shoots of the indigo plants, in contrast to the sun scorched land around the fields. After the excessive heat came the monsoon, and the rains began to fall in July.

Then the crops were cut. Each morning there would

be a line of carts drawn by the patient, slow-moving bullocks, carrying the indigo plants to the factory. Here the leaves were put into large vats where they were crushed until the juice ran from them. This liquid dye was then run off into lower vats where coolies stood, almost waist-high in the mixture, beating it unceasingly for two to three hours with long bamboo canes.

When the liquid slowly turned to a pulp it was pressed and cut into small cubes, stamped with the mark of the factory, and put on bamboo shelves to dry before being sent to the Calcutta markets.

William's scientific mind revelled in the needed exactitude to decide when the bundles of the plant had been fermented long enough in the upper vats and when to run the dark green liquid into the vats below. He learnt to watch the beating of this until it changed into an aquamarine blue; when to stop the beating and leave the liquid for the granules to settle before the water was drawn off. He had to watch the sediment, rich in value, being cleaned, boiled, strained and pressed, and he also had to know when it was dried sufficiently to be cut into cubes.

With his life-long interest in plant life of every kind, and its practical uses, he found a great fascination in the whole process.

Both the Mahipal and the Mudnabatty ventures were new outworks for George Udney. Indigo planters were being paid high prices and he was naturally anxious to get things going as quickly as possible. To secure that year's trade the indigo-making would need to begin by the middle of July so there was no time to be lost.

He agreed to pay Carey a salary equivalent to £250 yearly, a sum which was more than five times the amount he had ever received before. He could now not only be self-supporting but he would be able to put aside money for translation work.

Delighted, he wrote a letter to the headquarters in England: 'So I now inform the Society that I can subsist without any further monetary assistance from them. I sincerely hope that what was intended to supply my wants may be appropriated to some other mission. At the same time it will be my glory and joy to stand in the same near relation to the Society as if I needed supplies from them, and to maintain with them the same correspondence.'

He asked them to send out to him some tools with which to work the garden surrounding the new pukka two-storied house with large rooms and venetian windows which was to be their home. He also made a request for English flowering shrubs and fruit trees to be sent out to him each year: 'For the lasting advantage of what I now call my own country.' He longed to see an English garden growing in the heart of that land, and in the heart of her people he longed to sow the seed of love for the Christ he had come to tell them about.

There was an extra bonus in his new circumstances for he found in them a wonderful training-ground for future mission work. Constantly he tried to converse with his colleagues so that he would become more proficient in his knowledge and use of their language, and in discussions he was learning to see the Hindu and Islamic point of view more clearly. He had come to realize that this was vital if he were ever to do effective missionary pioneering. He lost no opportunity in presenting his colleagues with the gospel, and he found them ready to listen even though they showed no inclination to accept it.

The first season at Mudnabatty was going well and life for the Carey family seemed to have settled into a happier phase, when suddenly they were called upon to face a further sorrow.

Their five-year-old Peter became ill with a fever and inspite of all their tender nursing it became obvious that he was not going to recover. He died within hours, and in their lonely grief they found that none of the nationals wanted to take any part in the burial of one of the 'unorthodox dead'. They had to attend to everything themselves.

His duties at the factory took up much of Carey's time but they did not hinder him from pressing on with translation work. Before he had been in India a year he was able to write to Sutcliff: 'I intend to send you soon a copy of Genesis, Matthew, Mark and

James in Bengali. Also a small vocabulary and grammar of the language in manuscript of my own composing.'

He not only had to learn the language but the widely differing meanings of words and terms, but by the time the hook-swinging festivals came round again he was able to make himself understood as he protested boldly against these self-tortures.

His colleagues came to hear him preach on Sundays, but there were others there too, both Muslims and Hindus. In the afternoons he went out to the surrounding villages and preached in the open air. By tactful questioning he would get into conversation with a small crowd of people and, Indian nature being as curious as any other, a larger crowd would quickly gather. Then he would talk to them firstly about their gods and beliefs, showing his interest, until gradually he was able to lead them on to the message of salvation through Christ.

Carey ministered also to the Europeans living nearby, and a small Baptist church was founded at Malda. Here he delighted in the renewed fellowship with Thomas and frankly forgave him for the financial embarrassment he had caused earlier.

12

Letters from Home

It was a long time before William had a reply to his letter to headquarters in England. A stranger in a strange land, there was for him no twice-daily rattle of the letterbox but the frustration of waiting about eighteen months to receive an answer from home. It was all of that time before he heard from England and even then some of the news was far from encouraging. It seemed that one or two of the Committee were disturbed to know that Carey and Thomas were engaged in commerce and they felt this would detract from their true work. They spoke with solemn warning of danger: 'In the deceitfulness of riches.'

He who had advocated so strongly in his *Enquiry* the desirability of a missionary being self-supporting was stunned by their unwarranted rebuke. He replied, pointing out that had they done nothing to earn a living while they waited eighteen months for the first letter from home, they would indeed have been in a sorry plight.

William reminded them that he was maintaining

his missionary work out of his own income: 'I am indeed poor,' he wrote, 'and shall always be so till the Bible is published in Bengali and Hindustani, and the people need no further instruction.' He emphasized that no other line of business could have afforded him more leisure nor more opportunity of service. His employer not only permitted his missionary work, he backed it with his whole heart and will.

It was true of course that the Missionary Society was still a very new venture, and its members at home had as much to learn as its pioneer missionaries.

It was fortunate that there were other letters from home and these cheered Carey's heart as he pored over them. Fuller wrote giving detailed news of the other members of the missionary's family, and he also sent exhilarating accounts of the growing interest in the Mission among the home churches.

The Harvey Lane Church in Leicester was continuing to thrive, and Pearce wrote of spiritual as well as numerical development in the fellowship there. There was a spreading interest becoming apparent in many other places. Pearce added: 'At the recent Association Meeting at Kettering it would have done your heart good to have heard almost all the churches and ministers declare themselves revived in consequence of the Mission.'

This news came to the man in the forefront of the battle as cold waters to a very thirsty soul, reviving his spirit and encouraging him to go on attempting the great things for God in India on which his heart was so fixed.

It came also at a time when Carey most needed it. There was sadness in his home for his wife was becoming mentally sick. Katherine was not there to help her and she could no longer cope with ordinary domestic duties. To know that the wife he loved dearly was probably suffering as a result of the hardships the Mission had imposed on her was a hard cross to bear.

In 1796 the Mission found a new friend, Ignatius Fernandez, who had been trained for the priesthood by an Augustinian monk, with whom he had visited Bengal. He was so disturbed by the idol worship he saw there that he declined to take priest's vows, and after working ten years as a clerk built a large factory in Dinajpur for making candles.

Through reading a Portuguese Bible and discussing what he read with Thomas he had accepted Christ as Lord of his life. He built in his compound a preaching place for Indians and Europeans, and gave liberally to the interests of the Mission, keeping the missionaries supplied with honey, cloth and candles. The honey was sweet, the cloth was serviceable, but the candles were worth their weight in gold. Up till that time Carey had managed with only dim mustard-oil lamps for his nightly studies.

13

Translating the Bible

From the second year at Mudnabatty Carey devoted one third of his working day to the study of Sanskrit. It was India's status symbol; the criterion of her aristocracy. All her classics were enshrined in this sacred tongue, the speech of her soul and the ruling queen of her many dialects. He realized that to conquer it was to master the source of India's literature and the language used in their prayers.

He was fortunate to be introduced to the magistrate of Mirzapore, Mr H. T. Colebrooke, who had studied the Sanskrit language at Oxford. He was able to give Carey much help.

In April, 1796 Carey wrote to Ryland: 'I have read a considerable part of the Mahabharata, an epic poem written in most beautiful language and much on a par with Homer.'

With the study of Sanskrit he blended a considerable study of Hindustani until he could converse and preach in it, expecting that this would enable him to be understood over most of Hindustan.

He was also working hard at the Bible translation into Bengali, but this was a difficult and slow process. There were no Bengali prose classics to help him with their style, or the spelling of the language which was hopelessly uncertain. His pundit's style was stiff, and formal, and Carey's errors were often overlooked in a mistaken idea of politeness. However, he persisted and in the early part of 1797 he wrote exultantly: 'The New Testament is now translated into Bengali. Its treasure will be greater than diamonds.'

The books were not yet printed and to bring out the needed punches for this from England would cost about £4,000 for an edition of ten thousand copies. Floods had destroyed the crops for several seasons and the indigo industry was not flourishing. The two factories in the care of Thomas and Carey were not bringing in adequate returns. For this reason, and because of other losses, Mr Udney was now unable to help the Mission financially as much as he had hoped.

For a time, printing seemed an impossible task, but at the end of the year India's first commercial letter-foundry for vernacular types was established in Calcutta. Carey heard that they had a press there for sale at forty-six pounds. Mr Udney offered to buy this as a gift to the Mission. As soon as it was delivered printing began. An accomplishment to set the bells ringing in heaven!

During all this time Carey had never openly declared himself a missionary, for the East India Company were more resolute than ever to keep missionaries out of India. His work in the indigo factory classed him as a businessman and this fact satisfied the District Magistrate for the Bengal Government. If not, Carey would have been in constant danger of being expelled from the country and the very existence of the Mission would have been in jeopardy. For this reason he suggested to the folks in England that any new missionary coming out should come as an assistant to the factory.

One day William received an unexpected thrill. He was sitting at his desk with his pundit beside him, and as they were delving together into the mysteries of Sanskrit, there was an interruption. Carey looked up somewhat wearily from his book.

In the doorway stood a neighbour and with him another man, a stranger.

'Here is a man who comes from your country,' the neighbour explained. 'I met him twelve miles from here, enquiring for your house at Mudnabatty and so I brought him here. He will speak for himself.'

Carey rushed forward to shake hands with the stranger.

'Oh! But this is good! Welcome, my friend! Welcome indeed!' He continued shaking his hand: 'I can't tell you what it means to see one of my countrymen here, in this land of India. But why are you here? How did you come?'

'I am John Fountain.' He lowered his voice so that only Carey should hear. 'Here you see the new missionary, and the Mission's first recruit!'

'Ah! now I see. Some months ago they hinted in a letter from home that a new missionary may be coming some time, but to see you here on my doorstep, my friend, is almost too wonderful to be true.'

Turning to his pundit, he said: 'Put away my books. This has pleasantly spoilt my Sanskrit for today. My friend and I have much to talk over.'

William discovered that Fountain's home in England was in the county of Rutland, adjoining his own well-loved Northamptonshire. For a long time they talked together of the England they had left and the India of their adoption, and the hearts of both were warmed and uplifted.

The following weekend William took Fountain to see Thomas at Mahipal. In the services on Sunday, Fountain heard them both preach in Bengali as well as in English, with nearly a hundred people in the congregation.

It was an exciting day for all three missionaries, and at the end of it they raised their voices in heart-stirring community singing with songs of praises to Christ their Saviour. Fountain had a good voice they found, and before long a choir of thirty-six boys came into being under the musicianship of the Mission's first recruit.

14

Fresh Faces

Gradually, circumstances at the indigo factory began to change. The industry is dependent on good weather for its success and there had been several poor seasons before the final disastrous one.

It came suddenly. One day the workers went to the fields and found them covered with rice, hemp, indigo, cucumbers and gourds, with the promise of a rich crop. Then, without warning, the torrential rain poured down and within days there was not a vestige of anything to be seen but water, sometimes twenty feet deep.

With this catastrophe closely following his other losses, Mr Udney reluctantly decided to abandon Mudnabatty at the year end. Carey had to make plans to support his family, and preserve the existence of the Mission. He had now been in India for six years and most of the time he had struggled against difficulties. Here was a new crisis, but he refused to give up expecting the great things that had been promised. His side of the bargain was to go on attempting still more!

His licence in the indigo industry had three more years to run, and he would use this to help provide a business standing and a Mission settlement for new missionaries as they came out. For this purpose he used the money he had saved, together with a loan kindly offered by Mr Udney, to buy an indigo plant at Kidderpore, about twelve miles to the north.

Carey visualized that in this way missionaries could still come into the country as assistants at the factory and so by-pass the hostility of the East India Company. Eagerly, he began to build at Kidderpore in readiness and waited for further news from home in response to his appeal for more helpers to come out to India.

But the people in England did not fall in with Carey's wise and cautious planning. They refused to send out new missionaries to be registered as assistants for a factory.

This was unfortunate, for had they been able to agree to the arrangement, those who came out would have been allowed to enter Bengal as planters, and there would probably have been no complications.

Back in England there were five missionaries eager and ready to go to India with their families. One of them was the fiancee of John Fountain, who was already with Carey. The others were Marshman, Grant, Brunsdon and William Ward, the printer and journalist from Derby who had been interested in the Mission since he had talked with Carey seven years previously.

Fuller set about the almost impossible task of getting a passage for them all. He had hoped to hear of a Danish ship that could help in this, but found that all those going to India had already sailed.

He was beginning to give up hope of finding anything suitable when he discovered there was an American ship, the *Criterion*, just about to leave for Bengal. There was no time to lose. He went straight away for an interview with the Captain, explaining the position and asking for passages for the party of twelve.

Captain Wickes, a Christian man, readily agreed when he learned the reason for their going on such a voyage, and they sailed from Portsmouth on May 29th, 1799.

But all their problems were by no means solved. Charles Grant, now a Director of the East India Company, but still a keen enthusiast for the evangelization of the people of India, knew of his colleagues' bitter antagonism towards missionaries. Consequently, he advised the missionaries to avoid landing in Calcutta, where there was a possibility of their being banished immediately. He suggested they go direct to the Danish Settlement at Serampore, and with this in mind they carried with them a note of introduction from the Danish Consulate in London addressed to the Governor of Serampore, Colonel Bie.

When the boat anchored at the mouth of the Hooghly River, four months later, the harbour pilot boat lost no time in drawing up alongside. The pilot handed to the Captain the formal documents to be signed by each passenger, with full name and profession clearly stated. The passengers hesitated before signing, discussing with each other the problem this presented. They were young, eager and inexperienced, their lives committed to missionary pioneering and this was the sole reason for which they wanted to be admitted to this vast country.

It was true that Carey had wanted them to be registered as British citizens for the indigo factory staff personnel to ensure their admittance by the authorities. But in their hearts they knew their first responsibility was to bring the message of Christianity to the people of India. Finally, they felt unable to enter themselves on an official document as anything but missionaries on their way to the Danish Settlement of Serampore.

The papers were duly signed and as soon as they had been sent up to Calcutta, Captain Wickes gathered the passengers in his cabin. He told them of his concern: 'I approve of the firm stand you have taken over the signing of the papers, but I do not know what the outcome will be. One thing I do know is that you must not wait for a reply from the East India Company. It is advisable that you leave the boat and get to the Danish Settlement as quickly as possible.'

He then transferred the party with their baggage to two boats that were going upstream to Serampore, putting them in the care of his own Indian clerk who could speak a little English. He then wished them God-speed. It was all he could do.

When they reached Serampore they presented themselves to Colonel Bie, the Danish Governor, handing him the commendation they had brought. He received them kindly and offered to help in any way he could for the rest of their journey up country to join Carey, but warned them that it was possible the Company would not allow them to proceed.

This proved true enough for when the British authorities read the pilot's report and learnt these people had come as missionaries they immediately ordered them back.

Colonel Bie came to the rescue. He was a real friend in their desperate need. He continued to give them his fearless protection, and while they remained in his care at Serampore they would be beyond the jurisdiction of the British Government. He invited them to stay, and advised them to give a full explanation of their case to the Governor General, Marquis Wellesley, whose younger brother, Arthur, was later to become the famous Duke of Wellington, who distinguished himself as a military genius at the Battle of Waterloo.

Ward and Brunsdon requested an interview with the Governor General in Calcutta. They explained the situation carefully and finally convinced him that the missionaries' motives for coming to India were peaceful and humanitarian. Marquis Wellesley knew that they were in fact beyond his control while they remained at Serampore, and the meeting ended satisfactorily. The first crisis was over.

15

Serampore

The missionaries were tempted to stay at Serampore under the safe and friendly flag of Denmark, but they were also anxious to link up with Carey who was waiting for them at Kidderpore where he had made preparations. So when Fountain came to see them with a message from Carey begging them to press on they were ready to go. But the authorities were adamant and would not give way. Finally it was necessary for Fountain to return without them for further consultation with their leader and this time Ward went with him.

Carey was overjoyed to meet Ward again, but their reunion was tinged with sadness for already there had been a death among the new missionaries. Ward had to tell Carey that within three weeks of landing at Serampore Grant had been taken ill, and almost before it could be diagnosed the fever had proved fatal.

There was also good news for Ward to pass on to this brave pioneer who seemed to be having more than his share of setbacks. Colonel Bie had sent a message of comfort and encouragement, and an invitation to the missionaries to settle permanently at Serampore, where they should live as his 'honoured friends'. He offered to supply them with the necessary passports under his official seal for travel in British India.

In Serampore they could rent houses, establish schools, print and publish Scriptures as well as being free to preach in the church he was planning to build.

This was such a contrast to the attitude of the British towards missionary pioneering that it was hard to believe it could be true. Could any prospect be more alluring to a perplexed heart, burning with a desire to evangelize in the country of his adoption? Yet it was a large and dramatic step to take and needed some hard thinking before a decision could be made. Carey had to work this out alone, for his wife's illness had progressed so much that in her mental state she could not be consulted on any problem.

As the world stepped into the nineteenth century this great missionary pioneer was struggling with mountainous queries. He was baffled and confused. The opposition of the authorities of his native land grieved him continually and he was unable to understand their attitude. In contrast there was an invisible star surely added to the Danish flag.

By the time the New Year was ten days old Carey had made his decision, and on January 10th, 1800 he landed at Serampore. It had been necessary to cut his losses at Kidderpore, jettison his indigo factory there, incur a debt, and accept the courteous invitation of the Danish Governor to settle in his territory. Here, with God's help, he would build his Mission.

It added to the sadness of leaving Kidderpore that

he knew of no Indian who had yet accepted Christ's offer of salvation and new way of life. But he was leaving a crowd of zealous European Christians, and these he knew would carry on the work that he had begun.

Thomas by this time had drifted away. He had been so discouraged in the Mahipal works that he had given up the Mission and its worries. He travelled around with his wife and daughter from one place to another, sometimes living in a boat, then in a bamboo hut. Preacher, sugar-refiner, indigo worker, Thomas was definitely a rolling stone but was not altogether without his small garland of gathered moss.

16

The Settlement

Serampore was a small town on the west bank of the wide Hooghly River. Opposite was Barrackpore where the regiment of the East India Company's troops were quartered. The town that had given the strangers such a kindly welcome was not only an attractive one, but was becoming increasingly prosperous, wisely governed by Colonel Bie.

The well-ordered streets were busy, the river landing-places lively with the ships of many nations. This Danish port in Bengal would often see some two hundred large boats in full sail passing by in a tide. Calcutta was far enough away to cease to be a threat to the work of the Mission, but near enough to be reached in two hours when necessary.

Walking along the pleasant streets one could meet Danes, Germans, British, French, Portuguese, Greeks, Hindus, Muslims and Sikhs. Carey was impressed as he went on his first outing into the busy town and was reminded of the words of Christ: 'Many shall come from the east and the west, and shall sit down...in the kingdom of heaven' (Matthew 8:11).

Here was a mission field condensed into one centre with a world-wide appeal, a contact where more people could hear the gospel in a week than in six months at somewhere like Kidderpore. Brahmin influence was strong and the district was overwhelmingly Hindu. There had been Moravian missionaries working in the district from 1777 till 1792, but they had eventually given up the work without seeing any substantial results. The new missionaries had no illusions concerning the difficulties to be faced, but they looked beyond these to the ultimate great things God had promised.

Carey was convinced that a communal settlement was the best plan for a Mission's early years for the sake of economy, efficiency and essential fellowship. From the start he sought to knit the six families into one community, and he had good material to work on. Each person had their own particular gift to offer and the discerning leader was quick to discover what this was.

Ward, who was thirty, had been editor of the *Derby Mercury* and under his management it had become one of the chief English provincial papers. This was the man Carey had coveted for the printing of the Scriptures when he first met him seven years ago. Joshua Marshman, born within sight of the 'white horse' cut in the chalk of the Wiltshire hillside, had his thoughts first turned toward the East through reading accounts of the new Missionary Society. He was thirty-one; David Brunsdon was younger by nine years. Grant's widow and children were now naturally part of the missionary establishment.

The shoemaker of Northamptonshire was now a man of business experience, but the pulsating throb of his life was still to preach the gospel. It was his theme, his redeeming love. All he did was with this in mind and in an endeavour to further the cause.

Within a week of arriving at Serampore he had purchased a large well-built house which cost something like £600. He was resolved that the work should be based on a scale large enough to receive the great things he was sure would come.

In this large house there would be space to accommodate the missionary families. There would be a room for services to be conducted, another for the printing press, and still sufficient rooms left to run a school. The house was situated on the river bank, and with it was a piece of ground about two acres in size.

It was in this walled garden that Carey made a sanctuary arbour which he called his bower. It was the one place in all India that he kept exclusively for his own use, for personal Bible study and for the quiet times that would recharge his overworked 'batteries'.

Surrounded by the plants and flowers that gave him so much joy, he would seek and find the spiritual refreshment his soul longed for.

The money the new missionaries brought out with them was used to help meet the purchase price of the house. Bills on the Committee were drawn, and a loan raised in Calcutta to cover the balance.

When this was finalized they had £200 in hand and they hoped to increase this with earnings from the school they would eventually open.

The families had their separate apartments, but all met for meals in the one communal dining-room.

Arrangements were made for each family to receive a small personal allowance from the funds, and it was agreed that any money earned by the school, the press, or in any other way, should be paid into the Mission. The management of the household was to be taken by each in turn.

They realized that some misunderstandings were bound to arise when several families were living in such close proximity. Even in a Mission settlement! By facing up to this possibility they forestalled any festering grievances that might occur by setting apart every Saturday evening for frank discussion to settle any differences, and for renewing their pledge of fellowship.

It was important that they had an organized church life, so they constituted themselves a Baptist Church with Carey as Pastor, and Fountain and Marshman as Deacons. They accepted the Governor's invitation to conduct Sunday morning public worship in his house, and they continued to do this until the Danish Church building was completed in 1808.

It took a little time to set in order all these business matters, but when this was done they were able to give time to their individual tasks. Publication of the Scriptures was naturally their first concern, and Carey was helped in preparing the final copy and correcting the proofs by Fountain. Carey's son, Felix, now fifteen, was becoming increasingly useful and both he and his younger brother, William, knew Bengali almost as their native tongue.

Ward set himself to learn and master the script so that he could superintend the printing he was to do with the help of Brunsdon.

Marshman, who had acquired teaching experience in Bristol, undertook with the help of his wife to open boarding-schools for the children of wealthy Europeans and East Indians, one for the boys and the other for girls. These proved a great success from the start, the settlers were delighted to avail themselves of these educational facilities for their children. Before long the schools were earning more than £1,000 annually, and as time went on this amount was doubled.

But the missionaries were concerned about the other children in India who could not afford to pay fees, but needed the education they were unable to pay for. Within a month the Mission opened its third school, a free one, under the instruction of a Bengali master.

With the heart of the workers deeply embedded in their task it was not surprising that there was progress in each department. Ward and Marshman were quick to learn, and their devotion and capacity for the hard work involved were a continual joy to Carey. Mrs Marshman, one of the first women to be sent out as a 'missionary's wife', proved herself to be indeed a missionary in her own right, setting the example for the long line of courageous women who have followed her. It was said of Mrs Marshman that: 'Her heart was filled with sympathies, and her days with deeds of grace.' Colonel Bie continued to support the Mission in all its activities, and they never ceased to thank God for the kindness of this truly Christian gentleman.

It was soon after they had settled in at Serampore that they were surprised to see Thomas walking up to the door of the settlement house. Unpredictable as ever, he had decided to pay a visit to the Mission in their new quarters, and once there he stayed on to take his part and complete the missionary circle.

By March, the first page of the Bengali New Testament was pulled, giving zest and impetus to the translation work. The gold was beginning to show through after many years of hard and constant digging.

Thursday, April 24th, 1800 was kept as a Thanksgiving Day. This started with a sunrise prayer meeting, then a church meeting which officially called Carey to the pastorate, and this was followed by what would now be called a testimony meeting. Living in a foreign land, engrossed in a new work, it was refreshing for them to hear from each other how God had first spoken to them, and how they had responded to his offer of salvation through faith. In the evening Carey preached, taking as his text: 'Rejoicing in hope,' encouraging both himself and his listeners.

The arrival of letters from England was always the cause of great excitement, especially as this didn't happen very often. The fact that this time it coincided with Celebration Day provided its own 'Amen' to the jubilant thanksgiving.

17

Krishna Pal

Carey, with his colleagues, was now firmly established at Serampore, praying, teaching, preaching, translating, and, for an hour of each day, gardening. The preaching was not easy and it seemed sometimes that all was stony ground. Some listeners mocked and others remained aloof and disinterested. The Brahmins feared to break caste, even while they were intrigued by the preacher's knowledge of their Shastras.

More sadness came to the Mission when Fountain became ill with dysentery during the first year. He died on August 20th, 1800 and the native people were quick to taunt the missionaries. 'If God really sent you out to preach to us, why are two of your members dead already?' It was a question to which they could give no answer.

It was not until the end of the year 1800 that the Mission had its first convert, Krishna Pal. This was a man who had years ago done some carpentry work for the Moravian missionaries when they were in his area.

They had talked to him of Jesus Christ, the carpenter's son, but at that time Krishna Pal had not been interested. Now, when Thomas talked to him about salvation through faith in this same Jesus Christ, Krishna Pal responded and was ready to commit his life to God's leading. One had planted, another had watered, but God gave the increase.

The new convert began coming each day to the Mission to learn more, and what he heard he told to his wife and friends when he returned home. Their interest was roused and they too began to pay attention to Carey's message.

It wasn't easy for an Indian to become a Christian and confess this, and Krishna Pal had to face severe persecution. When he openly renounced idols and even joined the missionaries for a meal, the natives were outraged. A riot followed and two thousand people gathered in front of his house. The mob was eventually dispersed by order of the local magistrate, and a soldier was stationed outside the house to maintain peace.

The new convert was undaunted and he wanted to confess publicly the fact that he had accepted Christ as Lord of his life, so adult baptism was explained to him. As there had not yet been a baptism in India, Krishna Pal hadn't had the opportunity to witness the ceremony before, but he quickly understood that this was a way of identifying himself with his new Lord.

Felix, Carey's eldest son, wanted to be baptized at the same time so when the baptismal day arrived there were two candidates. It had been fixed for December 28th, 1800—the last Sunday in their first year at Serampore.

After much deliberation it had been decided to use the Hooghly River for the baptism, near the landing steps of the Mission house. As this river is actually one mouth of the Ganges the missionaries were careful to make it clear to the Hindus that they were using it solely on account of convenience for the Mission. It was not, they stressed, in any way because they recognized there to be any sanctity in the river itself.

This first baptism was a memorable day for the man who had worked for so long to tell the people of India something of the reality of God and the resurrection power of Christ to walk with certainty along the Christian path.

Early on that Sunday morning the missionaries gathered in their church to pray for blessing on this most important occasion. Outside there was a dense crowd of people; Hindus, Muslims and Europeans all eager to see what was going to happen. The missionaries walked through the crowd to the landing place where even more people were waiting. Governor Bie was there, with him a company of Danish and Portuguese Christians. Brunsdon, one of the missionaries who had been ill but was unwilling to miss the ceremony, was carried down to the river in a palanquin which was carefully placed near the water front by the four men.

Carey walked slowly into the water with his son and Krishna Pal on either side. He turned to address the vast multitude, explaining the meaning of the ceremony and what is involved when a person becomes a disciple of Jesus.

The crowd watched, still and silent, as the Hindu carpenter and then the English boy were immersed for a second under the waters of the Indian river. Carey spoke in English when baptizing his son; for Krishna Pal he spoke in Bengali.

When evening came there was a service of Holy Communion and for the first time this was administered in the Bengali language. The joy of the day was marred only by the fact that Dorothy, the mother of Felix, was unable to be present. Carey's dearly loved wife was by now permanently confined to her room.

Krishna's home soon became the halfway house to the Mission settlement. Native enquirers, too shy to approach the missionaries direct, would come first of all to ask for more details from the first member of their own people who had been brave enough to embrace these strange truths.

Other conversions followed and there were more baptisms as the new converts became fearless in re-

nouncing caste. They were persecuted, some even
losing their life for the sake of Christ. Carey emphasized from the start that he could not tolerate the idea
of new converts retaining their caste, but taught them
the truth that now they were 'all one in Christ Jesus'.
The caste system could no longer apply.

Early in 1803 the first Brahmin was baptized and
this naturally made a profound impression on the
Hindus. During the same year the first Bengali Christian wedding took place—that of Krishna's daughter
to the Brahmin convert. 'This,' wrote one of the
missionaries in their letter home, 'was a glorious
triumph over caste.'

Inevitably, the time came when the missionaries
were called upon to conduct their first funeral of a
Bengali Christian. The usual paid bearers were not
called in, to the amazement of the natives. They
watched in silence as they saw Marshman and Felix,
helped by a converted Brahmin and Mohammedan,
carry the coffin to its resting place.

The unity of all Christians, which Carey constantly
proclaimed, had now been demonstrated at Holy
Communion, at a marriage and at the graveside.

Meanwhile, translation was going forward. On
March 5th, 1801 the bound Bengali New Testament
was ready. Copies were sent to Fuller in England, and
a copy was graciously accepted by King George III of
England and also the King of Denmark.

But again as the work progressed there was further
sadness in the Mission settlement. The climate of
India which had caused Brunsdon's illness finally
overcame this brave man and he died on July 3rd,
1801, followed by Thomas three months later.

Only three of the seven missionaries were now left to carry on the work. It became more apparent than ever that Carey had been wise in his decision to establish the settlement as a community. For twenty-three years these remaining three, Carey, Ward and Marshman, worked together as a three-fold cord, each depending on the others and drawing strength from that fellowship. They became known as the 'Serampore Triad'.

With the base firmly established it was possible for the workers to consider a wider evangelism by itinerant journeys. Krishna Pal, in addition to his skill at carpentry, had a fluent tongue and a good share of natural ability, and Ward took him with him on the first tour. They travelled by boat to Deharta, visiting several towns on the way, meeting the people and talking with them. For the most part they were received well and the books and tracts they brought with them were eagerly accepted.

As well as these tours to take the gospel to the people in their own towns there were other enterprises undertaken at Serampore. Carey's two sons, Felix and William, helped by a faithful friend of the Mission, Ignatius Fernandez, opened the first Sunday School in India in 1803. There was little difficulty in getting the children in—more, maybe, in keeping their lively curiosity and high spirits in check!

18

College Lecturer

In 1801 the Governor General of India, Lord Wellesley, opened a new college at Fort William where young Civil Servants, sent out from England, could continue their education under supervision, and with the best possible tuition.

Throughout India, qualified men of learning were invited to come forward as candidates for posts of tutors, and there was a good response to this. The Rev. David Brown had been appointed Provost, and one of the most important Chairs was to be that of Bengali. Special care was needed in the selection of a suitable person to fill this vacancy.

When Carey received a letter from David Brown he was surprised. He was even more amazed to read the contents, asking him to come to Barrackpore to discuss a proposal for his appointment as professor of Bengali at the new college. This was an honour he had never contemplated, far less sought.

In his bewilderment he could do nothing before talking the matter over fully with his colleagues. They were delighted and saw in this a wonderful opportunity, not only for their friend but also for the furtherance of the whole aim of the Mission.

The students who would come under the teaching of Carey were the potential rulers in the land and his influence on them could be wide spread. Provided that the appointment would not hinder the work of the Mission they were convinced that Carey should be willing to accept the position. It could be of great service to the work the missionaries were seeking to do, for all the Eastern languages were to be taught in the college.

Accordingly Carey set off for an interview with Mr Brown and Mr Buchanan the Vice-Provost. When he arrived the first thing he asked them was how the appointment would affect the work of the Mission, stressing the fact that first and foremost he regarded himself as a missionary sent out to the people of India.

His interviewers assured him that they felt the interests of the Mission would be furthered rather than hindered. The Bengali New Testament would be introduced into the college, together with any other books Carey would recommend. He was overwhelmed at the wonderful prospect opening up before him.

Carey accepted the offered appointment. He later confessed: 'I was not able to reply to their arguments. I was convinced that it might be for the good of the Mission. As to my ability, they were not able to satisfy me, but they insisted that they must be the judges of that. I therefore consented with fear and trembling.'

At the start of his appointment he was given the status of lecturer only. The statutes of the college ruled that all professors on the faculty should be members of the Church of England, so Carey as a Baptist did not come into this category. As a lecturer he was paid a lower salary than a professor, but to the one-time cobbler the £600 per year they gave him seemed as a crock of gold!

When he took up his duties he stayed in Calcutta each week from Tuesday to Friday but was able to spend every weekend back at Serampore. In this way he was able to keep in vital touch with his colleagues and the work they were doing.

It would seem almost a miracle that a man born in a tiny English village, without any special schooling and with no college training, was now lecturing in an important college in a language he had only recently acquired. Carey had no idea of the ways of college life, no experience to draw upon, and in this way he still had much to learn.

After the first month he wrote to Dr Ryland: 'My ignorance of the way of conducting collegiate exercises is a great weight on my mind.' But there was no doubting his ability and before the end of the first term he was appointed teacher of Sanskrit, also. There were no books to help him. He had to create the literature he needed for his classes, and to compile grammar books for his pupils. When he delivered his first lecture there was not a single prose work in the Bengali language known to exist.

There were bound to be important effects on the Mission from this appointment. Financially, it made a considerable contribution to the income for they had a rule that any money earned privately by any mission-ary should be devoted to the general funds, and Carey was adamant in keeping this rule.

There was another advantage. The Mission now came under the protection of the flag of the East India Company. Lord Wellesley had gained complete confidence in Carey and no longer regarded him and his colleagues as a potential danger to Bengal.

In the college the new lecturer came into close contact with celebrated Indian pundits. He began to revise his Bengali Testament, drawing from the scholarship of these men and finding he was able to improve tremendously his first translation.

. There were also young Englishmen in the classes training for the Civil Service, and his missionary heart warmed towards these representatives of the country he had loved and left.

Carey had been on the staff of the college for about nine months when Lord Wellesley instituted an enquiry into the atrocities committed in the name of religion, such as the sacrifice of infants to the Ganges, and 'Sati'—the burning of widows on the funeral pyres of their husbands.

Carey was asked to investigate the Hindu principles upon which these practices were based—his knowledge of the Sanskrit language giving him a valuable insight into the sacred books of the country. He welcomed the task, and recognized it as one of vital importance to the liberation of the country, and people, of his adoption. When his results were disclosed the Governor General made the sacrifice of children a heavily punishable crime.

Carey went on to ask for the freedom of slaves, and to continue to plead for the abolition of 'Sati' which caused the untimely death of about ten thousand widows annually. They were horrors that had torn at his heart for many years.

But it was to be more than another twenty years before the religious prejudices of the natives could be sufficiently overcome to enable the Governor to make 'Sati' illegal.

The Fort William College had its share of good and not so good students, but all were touched by the Christian influence of the energetic and painstaking tutor who saw in his work facets of missionary enterprise.

At the annual College Disputation in 1804 Lord Wellesley asked for the principal address to be given in Sanskrit as the course had now been going for three years.

For this event the magnificent throne-room of Government House was packed with the cream of Calcutta's learning. There in their appointed place were the Chief Justices and the Judges of the Supreme Court, members of the Council, commercial magnates and distinguished members of the civil and military communities, including the future Duke of Wellington.

Dotted about among these dignitaries were Indian princes dressed in their exquisite Oriental silks, sparkling with jewels; many scholastic pundits, notable Brahmins, and in fact all the wealth and learning of the country was represented.

There was a hush in the vast room as Carey entered. With a quiet dignity he stood before them all and requested them to be seated. Conquering his natural nervousness he introduced his subject. Then, using the ancient classic tongue of India, he delivered the first Sanskrit speech ever to be given by a European.

He sat down when he finished and furtively wiped the perspiration from his bald head!

In 1806 Carey was granted the full title of professor and his salary increased to £1500 a year. All this he consecrated to the promotion of Christianity in India.

How his work flourished and his true worth became recognized in the college is shown by the fact that through thirty years nothing was established under official patronage in Bengali, Marathi and Sanskrit without his endorsement.

Yet through it all this humble man remained ever a student himself, learning from his pundits some new Indian tongue to add to his ever-expanding repertoire.

It was little wonder that his great love of all that was based in India's literature and life, drew Indian people to him, and made him their friend.

19

'Great Things'

The staff at Serampore had been increased by five more missionaries, and in 1805 Felix was formally accepted as an active member of the settlement. More and bigger property was eventually bought, and again this was vested in the Society.

Though the settlement was now on a financially sound basis the members continued to live as economically as possible. The Marshmans drew a yearly sum of only thirty-four pounds from the thousand pounds the school was producing. From the proceeds of the press the Wards had twenty-four pounds, and out of his college salary Carey retained forty pounds to keep his wife and three sons, with an extra twenty to enable him to appear in college suitably dressed!

The Bengali Old Testament was published in sections between 1802 and 1809. The people of India could now read in their own language stories of Abraham, Jacob, Joseph and Elijah. They could thrill to the story of their own Ahasuerus and Esther, his

WILLIAM CAREY: BY TRADE A COBBLER

queen. They could read of the 'ivory, apes and pea-cocks' which were sent in ships to adorn the court of the opulent King Solomon, and perhaps wonder in their hearts whether these could indeed have been sent from their own land.

They would read in the New Testament of One who said: 'A greater than Solomon is here.' And they could begin to believe that when Jesus also said: 'Come unto Me,' he included the people of India in his invitation.

The settlement hoped to expand by opening new mission stations about a hundred miles apart, each one to be put in charge of an English missionary. Around these stations they would set up out-stations under the care of Indian Christians.

Exciting plans were made for this development of the work, but once again they found themselves opposed by the Government who were not convinced that the work of the missionaries would not cause a disturbance of the lethargic peace: 'We do not think it wise to interfere with the prejudices of the nationals,' they said.

Then came the tragic news of a massacre at Vellore near Madras which sent a warning sound throughout India.

On July 10th, 1806, Sepoys had made a vicious attack on the European garrison, killing over a hundred men. The mutiny was sudden and unexpected, carried out without warning.

Those who opposed the idea of evangelizing were quick to seize on this tragic news, suggesting the mutiny was a result of missionary work. It had, they said, caused alarm to the nationals who suspected that the Government was seeking to convert them forcibly.

There had been no missionaries in Vellore, or its district, and the accusation was in any case a wild, extravagant one, made at a time of panic, and without any logical evidence.

When the story reached England the Directors of the East India Company investigated it, but their enquiries proved that the Vellore massacre had nothing whatever to do with missionary work. There were still, however, those in England who were not convinced.

Friends of the Mission both in India and in England took up the cause. The Marquis of Wellesley, as he now was, had retired as Governor General of India, but he was still a friend of the Mission and used his influence as far as possible. The storm abated and there was a short lull until the middle of 1807 when the new Governor General, Lord Minto, took up his duties. The anti-missionary party did their utmost to persuade him that Carey and his colleagues were a danger to the State.

Greatly daring, however, Carey and Marshman called on him and presented a copy of the translation of the great Hindu sacred epic 'Ramayana' as evidence of the kind of Oriental studies they were engaged in. Lord Minto listened graciously to their explanation of the missionary work and its aim. They were able to tell him about a hundred Indians, including twelve Brahmins, sixteen men of the writer caste, and five Muslims who had been baptized on confession of their faith.

Lord Minto was favourably impressed and promised to study the matter in detail before submitting it to his Council who, on his recommendation, agreed to allow the press to continue their publications, and the missionaries to preach.

But the missionary conflict went on in England for two or three more years. The leaders of the movement made a united effort to petition Parliament to allow missionaries to be sent to India to work among the natives.

When the Company's Charter came before the House in 1813 the following clause was incorporated: 'That it is the duty of this country to promote the interests and happiness of the British dominions in India, and that such measures ought to be adopted as may tend to the introduction among them of useful knowledge and of religious and moral improvement: that in the furtherance of the above sufficient facilities shall be afforded, by law, to persons desirous of going to and remaining in India, for the purpose of accomplishing these benevolent designs.'

Cheers went up when they heard the Bill had received the Royal Assent. India was officially open to missionary enterprise and the missionaries need no longer furtively steal in by the back door! From God they had expected; for God they had attempted. Now the 'Great things' were coming to pass!

20

Busy Times

Translating, printing and publishing went on at such a pace in Serampore that people began to ask how three men could translate into so many languages.

'Few people know what may be done till they try, and persevere in what they have undertaken,' was Carey's adept answer to their query.

Little did anyone appreciate how many times a translated work had to be corrected, revised and re-written before it satisfied the discerning mind of the translators. New editions followed, one after the other.

To acquire so much knowledge of the different languages it was necessary to study and write out the grammer of each of them, full as they were of irregular peculiarities. These grammars Carey published as they were finished.

In such a vast, wide field of adventure into which they had plunged—the languages of the Orient—it was inevitable that mistakes would be made, but this fact was faced with courage as Carey and Marshman pressed on, revising and improving right to the end of the chapter.

They found that the Bengali Old Testament was well received by the middle-class people, but the Brahmins scorned a book in the vernacular of the common people. They considered no book worthy to be called sacred which was not written in their ancient Sanskrit.

It was when Carey realized this fact that he set about translating the books of the Bible into this classic, religious and literary tongue of India. It was the root of most of the modern vernaculars of the country, and by mastering it he found the key to unlock possibilities of translation on a much wider scale than he had previously dreamed about.

He was overjoyed to find that when his Sanskrit editions were printed the Brahmins were quickly attracted to the Scriptures. Eventually there was a translation of the whole Bible into Sanskrit; and then his fertile mind tingled with the prospect of tackling all the chief Oriental languages in turn.

When, in 1804, the British and Foreign Bible Society came into being in London, an auxiliary was formed in Bengal with the Serampore Triad as members of the Committee. When the Bengal Committee settled down to planning their programme, it agreed to pay the Mission 300 rupees a month to assist them in their translating.

Further gifts of money came from England and the United States. Gradually, book by book, came the Old and the New Testament in Sanskrit, Orissa, Maharati, Hindustani and Gujarati, Carey being the master translator, helped by Marshman.

The amazing achievements of the Serampore Press

were made possible by an excellent team backing their able and energetic leaders. At the Mission head-quarters they now employed an enthusiastic body of pundits who wrote out rough translations of the books on which Carey and Marshman were engaged. These they compared with one another, to iron out the difficulties they encountered in the various languages, and dialects, before passing them over to the leaders. Then they corrected press proofs and manuscripts, making a valuable contribution to the whole work of translation.

These were busy days for everyone involved, not least for the indomitable Carey, the 'workaholic'! He would be at work by six in the morning, after a short time for private devotion, followed by family prayers in Bengali for the servants. A quick break for *chota hazari* (little breakfast) before settling down to the translation of the moment. At ten o'clock he would be off to the College where his classes kept him till two in the afternoon. Back at his lodgings there would be Sanskrit translation and a study of one of the other languages he was learning. His day was not yet over, he would then preach in English to some forty people and when the congregation had dispersed he would fill in two hours on the Bengali translation, write a letter to a friend in England, and read a 'goodnight' message from his Greek New Testament, before probably just tumbling into bed! This was not an exceptional but a typical day in the life of the one-time country cobbler who set his mind, even as he cobbled, on evangelizing the world.

So the work went on its missionary way with Carey ever seeking fresh fields to conquer by way of language and dialect—his zealous heart never satisfied as long as he could see there was still more land to be possessed.

His Bengali version was the one that lay nearest to his affection and he continued to revise it, not feeling that his work on it was finished until he had read the proofs of his eighth and final edition.

21

Calamity

While the work was progressing as far as the translations were concerned, there were still many problems to tackle at Serampore in the printing departments. They had a wide field to cover, for their work included not only the Scriptures but many of the sacred books of India. One of these was *The Sanskrit Dictionary of Amara Sinha*. To begin with, there was no printing type available in the various languages into which these books were being translated.

At first the missionaries were in despair, and felt rather like the Israelites of old who were commanded by the taskmasters of Egypt to make bricks without the essential commodity, straw! Help came at last from an unexpected quarter, when they found a man who had learnt the art of cutting punches for casting type from the printer, Sir Charles Wilkins. Ward immediately sought his help and together they were able to build a letter-foundry. This eventually became the chief foundry for Oriental type in Asia.

But as the list of translations became ever larger,

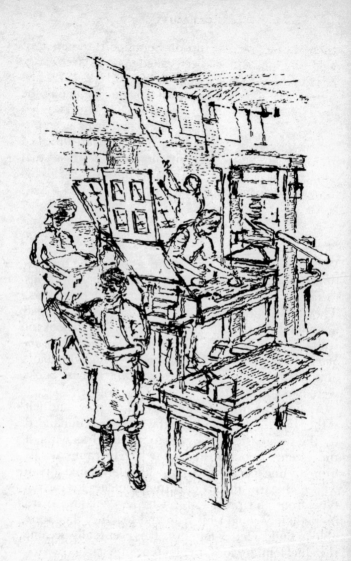

there came creeping up on Serampore the greatest calamity they had yet been called upon to face.

It was a hot, dry evening on March 11th, 1812. The Serampore Press had closed for the day, and the Indian employees had gone home. Only Ward was left in the office where he was busy preparing accounts before locking up the building. He had nearly finished the last one when suddenly he raised his head and looked round. Was there a smell of burning? He lost no time in going to investigate.

Beyond the long composing room there was another room where paper was stored. Twelve thousand reams of it, and it was from that room that the ominous smoke was trailing through.

'Fire! Come quickly!' he shouted, knowing there were one or two servants still around outside.

They rushed to Ward's assistance, calling to others on the way, their shouts bringing Marshman running from the house. Carey, of course, was away at the College.

'Close all windows and doors, and keep them shut.' Ward shouted. He realized that every effort must be made to localize the fire and prevent it from spreading to the main building.

He climbed up the outside steps and frantically hacked away a large hole in the flat roof immediately above the fire. Indians, Europeans, servants, and neighbours quickly gathered, forming a human chain to bring water from the nearby river in large earthenware 'chatties'—brass pots—and any suitable vessel they could find. The water was constantly poured on to the fire, everyone working fiercely for about four hours while the paper inside the room smouldered.

Brave volunteers managed to rescue some of the Deeds, records and other valuable papers from the office. Five presses with a frame of type on each were miraculously brought out from the printing room.

The workers were exhausted, but greatly relieved that they had been able to keep the fire from spreading to other rooms. They knew that the large stock of paper would go on smouldering for some hours, although it appeared that danger to the rest of the building was now past.

Then tragedy struck. Among the large crowd watching the proceedings was someone, over-eager to help, who decided to open one of the windows. A draught of air swept through the building like a pair of bellows, and huge flames shot up from the embers as they were rekindled. Now the fire quickly reached the composing-room, and in a matter of seconds the whole place was an inferno.

Oriental, Greek, Hebrew and English type blazed to ashes together with proofs, printed sheets and a thousand copies of the first sheets of Henry Martyn's Hindustani Testament which had just come off the press. Precious manuscripts of Scripture translations, grammar and other books, representing many months of intensive study and hard work crumpled like tissues in the heat. The workers who had fought the fire with frenzied energy were at last beaten.

Not till the morning light revealed the extent of the damage could the downcast group of helpers see how devastating it was. They were appalled.

Marshman went off to Calcutta to inform Carey of the disaster, leaving Ward behind at the scene of destruction. After a short rest he gathered his helpers together again, and they searched for anything that might be salvaged from the smouldering ruins. After many hours working among the debris, collecting fragments of half-burned books and damaged papers, their hands were sore, their bodies racked with exhaustion and their hearts aching with the desolation of it all.

But when they had cleared the place where the machine-room had been, there was a great shout of joy. They found that the valuable punches and the matrices of all the Indian types were practically undamaged. This was little short of a miracle to those who had witnessed the fire last night. To everyone it was a profound relief.

Carey arrived with Marshman in the evening and inspected the scene of destruction, then immediately discussed with his colleagues plans for repairing the damage, and restarting production. It was a calamity but they were not in despair. They were still eager to continue, encouraging themselves by remembering it was *after* the fire that Elijah heard the 'still small voice' and knew that God was there.

No time was lost, and the following day casting began on the molten metal which they had been able to collect from the floor of the burnt-out building.

Some of the precious manuscripts were never replaced; the dictionary based on the Sanskrit which Carey had laboriously prepared, and the translation of the Ramayana, were two of these.

Carey wrote to Fuller in England: 'The loss is heavy, but as travelling the road a second time, however painful it may be, is usually done with greater ease and certainty, so I trust the work will lose nothing in real value.... The work is already begun again in every language.'

It was natural that there was considerable concern among the people in England when they learnt of the catastrophe, and their sympathy was shown in a practical way. In less than two months a sum of £10,000 was raised toward the cost of repair.

It had been a shattering experience but from it the missionaries had learnt much. Carey found that as he rewrote the versions that had been destroyed he was able to improve on them. The Oriental type was all remade in six months and by the end of a year the Mission press was in a more efficient state than it had been before.

By 1832 complete Bibles, New Testaments, or separate books of Scripture had been issued in forty-four languages and dialects. This was a task representing team work at its highest level.

22

Christian College

The year was 1813 and William Carey was now fifty-two years old, a college professor, a man of proven business acumen, translator, printer and established publisher. But at the heart of this great man was his love of India and her people, and his longing for the Christian message to reach from end-to-end of her vast domain. This was the vision that had come to him all those years ago in his shoe-making workshop, and it never grew dim but remained like a beacon light to the end of his days.

As the years passed the Mission staff grew steadily larger, with something like thirty workers, Indian and European, and its twelve stations were scattered over Upper India, Bengal, Burma, Orissa, Java and Mauritius.

This expansion of the work, though a constant joy and encouragement to those actively engaged in it, was looked upon with a certain apprehension by those at the home base in England. Expenses were naturally rising with every new project, and they suggested that it might be wiser to slow down instead of pressing ever forward.

But to Carey and his colleagues this attitude of restricting the work to fit the present income was all wrong. Their policy was to make every effort to increase finances so that they met the demands that the work of God requested from them. Results that were following the expansion movements were proving to them that this was God's way of bringing blessing. People were being converted to Christ and the number of adult baptisms was rising annually.

In 1814 the new Governor General, Lord Moira, who was in sympathy with missionary work, visited Serampore with his wife and the newly appointed first Bishop of Calcutta. This was a great honour and it proved to be a day of heart-warming encouragement to the workers there, for the three visitors were all very much impressed by what they saw. They were told about the recently developed scheme for opening vernacular schools in the villages in connection with the Mission Station, where Indian teachers were put in charge, with a monthly visit from one of the missionaries.

Lord Moira had heard of this scheme previously and he had backed it from the start, regarding it as Britain's duty to pass on sound Western knowledge to Indian young people. Now he heard that a band of teachers had been trained in the new method of schooling and that there were nineteen schools in the villages around the Station.

At the annual speech day of Fort William College in July 1817 Lord Moira (by now the Marquis of Hastings) gave voice to his views. In his speech he emphasized: 'It is human, it is generous, to protect the feeble; it is meritorious to redress the injured; but it is a God-like bounty to bestow expansion of the intellect .... It would be treason against British sentiment to imagine that it ever could be the principle of this government to perpetuate ignorance in order to ensure paltry and dishonest advantages over the blindness of the multitude.' Within a year forty-five schools had been opened.

Still the beacon light called them on, and the success of the schools project encouraged the missionaries to take the next step. For some time they had been considering the idea of establishing a Christian College at Serampore. The aim would be to give a more advanced education to young Indians, particularly those of Christian parentage. Years of work had taught the pioneers the importance of education in their Christian churches, and they were now convinced that India could best be won for Christ by Indian people.

Indian workers had for a long time been helping the missionaries by teaching and preaching, but Carey felt they needed further training. They needed to become familiar with the doctrine they would teach, and this could only be attained by a complete study and knowledge of the Scriptures. As Indians they would already be familiar with the doctrines they would need to combat, but would be better equipped by learning more of the dogmas which form the core of the Buddhist and Hindu systems.

Plans went forward and on July 15th, 1818 the Mission issued a prospectus of a proposed 'college for the instruction of Asiatic, Christian and other youth in Eastern literature and European science'.

A piece of land was bought to the south of the Mission premises and their old friend, the Danish Governor, accepted the position of first governor of the college. Lord Hastings readily agreed to become the First Patron of Serampore.

At first an old house on the new land was used for the college and thirty-seven students enrolled. Nineteen of these were professed Christians, fourteen Hindus and four stated on their enrolment form 'no caste nor religion'.

The missionaries started off the building fund with £2,500 out of their earnings. Lord Hastings gave 1,000 rupees, and many others contributed as they were able.

The new building rose brick by brick until in 1821 Serampore College was a dream come true. It had cost £15,000, and it was voted one of the noblest European buildings in Asia.

There was a wonderful sense of space and strength in every part of this new venture and the extensive

grounds around the college leading right down to the wide Hooghly River added their share in its attractive appearance.

His Majesty, the King of Denmark, sent a personal letter to Carey and one to Marshman, expressing his appreciation of the work they were doing. He enclosed a gold medal for each of them in place of the offered honours they had previously declined.

The King of Denmark also made a gift to the college of a large house and grounds which adjoined the college, and this became a valuable addition to the buildings.

In 1827 His Majesty, who had retained his keen interest in the work and progress of Serampore College, granted a Royal Charter which gave power to the college to confer on its students 'degrees of rank and honour according to their proficiency'. This meant that Serampore College was the first one in Asia to be able to offer degrees to its students.

During all the excitement of new ventures Carey often remembered his tiny study in the attic of the cottage in Leicester, where his ideas had been fertilized in the warm throbbing of a heart burning with enthusiasm. His determination had widened an already wide vision. He had expected, attempted, and was now experiencing the great things he had longed for.

But once again people at the Society's headquarters in England were not in full agreement with the methods for progress used by the missionaries. They did not know all the problems and they could not understand the ultra-modern outlook of the Serampore trio. Over a distance of 15,000 miles it is possible for the most worthy men to be misjudged and the highest motives suspected. From that distance away the people in England could see Carey only through the haze of thirty-four years. To many of the younger members of the Committee he must have been a name only. They had never met him and did not know the man himself.

It was decided that Ward should have a break from his printing and make a return visit to England to meet personally the critics and their criticisms. He would be able to give first-hand information about the new college and discuss with the Committee the further plans that were in the pipeline. He achieved little, and returned to India disappointed but more determined than ever to add his own weight' to the Serampore work and purpose. Four years later he became ill with cholera and died at the age of fifty-three. This first break in the trio imposed a heavy burden on the remaining two members, adding to their sorrow at losing their devoted colleague.

In 1827 Marshman visited England and put the case for Serampore clearly before the members of the Committee. They did not feel able to give their support to all the projects that were contemplated, and a breach became inevitable. After full discussion Marshman reluctantly signed an Agreement of Separation, which stated that he and Carey were to be left in charge of the College at Serampore and the grounds attached to it. The older missionary property was to be vacated and put in the hands of the Baptist Missionary Society Committee. In due time younger missionaries would be sent out to take the place of the Serampore staff.

These were the details of the arrangement and Marshman travelled back to Carey with the news. For both of them it was a hard blow to bear, and the break from the Society Carey had himself founded was not healed during his lifetime. But in 1855, on Marshman's last visit to this country, the college came back under the Society, a move welcomed by everyone.

Preparations were made for what Carey, with his Northamptonshire background, still called a 'flitting'. The press and the plant belonging to the original Mission, and the personal possessions of the staff were packed up and transported from their familiar surroundings to the college site.

Outside the claims of the Committee, Serampore was now separate from the Baptist Missionary Society.

23

The Family Man

Over the years Carey the pioneer, the lover of India and her people, never neglected his own family and their interests. He remained devoted to his wife and his sons, and when he feared his busy life might be depriving them of his personal time and attention he would write them a letter to show that he cared. These had to be written late at night after his official duties were finished and the family were all tucked up in bed. The letters assured his sons of their father's love and interest.

Like any parent he had plans for their future, and as the years went by he endeavoured to have each of them suitably trained and fitted for their chosen career.

Dorothy Carey never fully recovered from her mental illness and for twelve years Carey nursed her, giving her all the love and devotion of his heart. He never forgot the sacrifice she had made in following him, albeit fearfully, to the ends of the earth, leaving for ever her own country and kindred.

Dorothy never left the Mission settlement and in

her last days she was still surrounded by her family and the many faithful friends in the Mission house. She died in 1807.

Forlorn in the isolation that comes with the loss of a life partner, Carey found some consolation in the continuance of his college and missionary work, but after a time he met, loved and married a second wife.

Charlotte Rhumohr, who was about the same age as William, was from a family in the Duchy of Schlesing which had been able to give her the blessing of a good education. Carey was overjoyed when he found she could speak Danish, German, French, Italian and English equally well.

Early in life Charlotte had come to India and had a house built for herself in Serampore, where she and William eventually met. A cultured, Christian lady, she was admirably suited to become the wife of a master linguist. And for thirteen years she proved to be a true help-meet, sharing the work, the joys and the trials that come to a college lecturer, translator, missionary or housewife! Charlotte's love and devotion made these years a period of sheer happiness, and her death in 1821 caused her husband one of his greatest sorrows.

The following year brought another grief to Carey when Felix, his eldest son, died at the age of thirty-six. News from England told him of the passing away of many relatives and friends and in a downcast mood he wrote: 'Everything dear to me in England is now removed. Wherever I look I see a vast blank.... However I never intended to return to England when I left it, and I shall not do it.... My heart is wedded to India, and though I am of little use, I feel a pleasure in doing the little I can.'

In his loneliness he met and married his third wife, kind and thoughtful Grace Hughes, a widow seventeen years his junior. They were happy in their companion-ship and as William grew older she cared for him lovingly.

24

'Sati' Abolished

It was Sunday, December 5th 1829, and Carey was up early in his study at Serampore, preparing his mind for the pulpit where he was due to preach.

The morning quiet was broken by the sound of the doorbell and he went to investigate. The unexpected caller was a courier from the recently appointed Governor General, Lord William Bentinck, and the message was an urgent one. The letter asked Carey to translate immediately into Bengali the enclosed Order in Council.

Not too pleased to be disturbed on a Sunday morning by a request to translate a Government Edict, he began to read the document, but what he read quickly removed the frown from his forehead and set heaven's bells ringing for William Carey.

This Edict was the result of something he had been campaigning for ever since his earliest days in India. It was the now famous document for the abolishing of 'Sati' throughout the British Dominions.

Like a schoolboy who has just been told he has won

a coveted prize, Carey sprang from his chair, threw off the black jacket he wore when studying, and sent a request to one of his colleagues to take his place at the services that day.

With no more delay he settled down with one of his pundits for the momentous task of the translation. After years of urging the Government to take this vital life-saving step, nothing must now be allowed to hinder its completion. No widow should die on the funeral pyre of her husband because William Carey was too slow in translating the Edict which would save her.

He spent the whole Sunday on his task and by evening the translation was finished and on its way back to the Governor General. Mercifully for the vast majority of Indian widows the ceremony of 'Sati' became a custom which fell into disrepute, although there are still rare instances where a widow insists on being cremated on the funeral pyre of her dead husband.

Gradually, India became open to missionaries and Carey was able to meet more representatives from other churches who came out to the mission field. He delighted in meeting them and found this added fellowship a source of more blessing.

One of the men he met in this way was Alexander Duff, a young Scotsman who had arrived at Bengal in the Spring of 1830. On a hot, July day he called at Serampore and asked to see Carey who was in his study on the verandah overlooking the river. After the usual greetings were over the older man listened with eager interest to this enthusiastic young missionary who was bubbling over with plans for an educational mission.

He explained that his ideas had not favourably impressed the missionaries with whom he was working, and he had travelled to Serampore with the hope of discussing them with an understanding and experienced listener.

The young man was someone after Carey's own heart and he welcomed him and his scheme with sheer joy. At the end of the interview Alexander Duff went on his way rejoicing indeed, encouraged to press on with his plans knowing he had the approval and blessing of the wise veteran of Serampore.

25

Pensioned Off

The end of one road does not necessarily see the end of all problems, and for William Carey the road wound uphill most of the way.

The Serampore Mission was dependent on their own earnings and gifts from their friends in India. In 1830 when the financial crisis arose in Calcutta several of their most wealthy supporters were seriously affected, making it impossible for them to contribute to the Mission as previously.

A further blow came when the Government, burdened with the strain of the colossal expense of the war in Burma, was obliged to apply economy at home. One of the victims of the recession this caused was the Fort William College. It was forced to abolish the professorships. With others, Carey knew the sinister meaning of redundancy, and he was pensioned off on about £360 a year.

He had always lived frugally and this amount was more than enough for his personal needs, but it meant that the salary he had been receiving for almost thirty years and which had been the most important source of support for the Mission, was no longer there.

Then, in 1833, came even more financial ruin to some of the businesses in which part of the funds of the Mission were invested.

These monetary trials naturally put a great strain on the man who had for seventy-one years been living out his strength at a maximum rate, and he was greatly troubled by it all. But his faith remained as firm as ever. The God he had expected to do great things was still there.

To the great relief of the staff the immediate needs of the Mission were taken care of by one of their generous friends, and when news of the financial catastrophe reached England, the people there rallied round. The emergency was met and eventually the crisis passed.

With the closing down of the professorships Carey now had to adjust to a life without his involvement with Fort William College, to which he had been devoting half his time for the last thirty years. His leaving was a traumatic experience both for himself and other members of the staff there. His Indian pundits gathered round to offer condolences as much for themselves, as for their loved professor who was leaving them. He was intensely moved by their expression of appreciation and his heart was heavy as he bid them a final goodbye.

He missed his daily visits to Fort William and it wasn't easy to settle down but, never a man content to sit and twiddle his thumbs, he threw himself more ardently than ever into the work at Serampore College. He was responsible for the lecturing in divinity and his other favourite subject, natural history. On Sundays he continued to help with the services in the church and also did his share of preaching, sometimes in Bengali, sometimes in English.

Though there was never any question of him needing to lose weight as he was always slight, he took plenty of exercise—leaving the house early each morning for a ride of several miles before returning at sunrise for breakfast.

The translation work was, of course, always there. During his retirement he decided to start on yet another revision of his Bengali New Testament. The man who had been busy all his days continued to be something of a 'workaholic', albeit a contented one, refusing to allow the listlessness of the tropics to interfere with his sense of mission.

Carey had passed through deep waters of sadness in his pilgrimage and, like all men of a sensitive nature, he had his times of sheer black depression. Gradually though, the clouds would lift and his inborn optimism take over once more. Marshman wrote of Carey at this time: 'He is cheerful, and happy as the day is long!'

26

An English Daisy

Despite all his other activities William Carey maintained his childhood passion for plants and flowers, memorizing their Latin names and studying their characteristics. The man who wrestled in a strange land with the intricacies of Oriental languages never lost his love for the simple wonders of nature.

Encircling his missionary and translation work he made for himself a garden soon after settling at Serampore, and here he was able to develop his hobby. He laid out the five acres with the skill of an expert, and with such meticulous care that within a few years it became one of the finest botanical collections in Asia. He loved the exotic wild flowers and trees of India and endeavoured to have at least one of every kind in his garden.

There was the Indian Liquorice with its spike of small pink flowers and its beautifully coloured seeds which the nationals used as beads and made into necklaces. He planted black pepper and the magnificent dhak tree whose flowers come out before its leaves and make a wonderful show in the early Spring.

In the wide borders there were crimson rhododendrons, the hibiscus shrub and, growing against the walls of the garden, the bougainvilia with its pink, mauve or bright orange flowers. In the evenings the white flower of the 'Queen of the Night' would open out to fill the air with its fragrance.

Later in the year there was the poinsettia making its own floral pattern with its large scarlet leaves. An assortment of plants as varied and colourful as the life of the man who cultivated them.

But never could these blot out from Carey's mind the plants and flowers he had loved in his native land. Soon after he arrived in India he requested friends in Britain to send out to him seeds of violets, cowslips, stately foxgloves and hollyhocks, and bulbs of the winter snowdrop, crocuses, etc. Even the thistles and nettles that creep unwanted into an English garden were to Carey in India some of the precious reminders of home to be taken care of. They grew among the rare and beautiful plants of India like a symbol of national unity.

One day as he walked in his garden he discovered a speck of white growing among the seeds he had scattered. He stooped to examine it and found it to be the generally despised daisy that is quickly uprooted if it appears on an English lawn, but to Carey it might have been a diamond glistening there. Later in the day he wrote to friends at home: 'I know not that I ever enjoyed, since leaving Europe, a simple pleasure so exquisite as the sight of the English daisy. I had not seen one for over thirty years.'

Even in his hobby the welfare of India was upper-

most in his mind, and he believed it could be utilized
for the good of her people by forming a Horticultural
and Agricultural Society. He put the idea before lady
Hastings, wife of the Governor General, and he was so
encouraged by her keen interest in the scheme that he
went ahead.

On September 14th, 1820 the Society came into
being under the patronage of her husband, Lord
Hastings. Within a few weeks of its formation it had
grown to a membership of fifty.

Two years later Carey was elected a Fellow of the
Linnean Society in London, and a member of both the
Geological and the Royal Horticultural Society.

In 1833 he was elected President of the Agricultural
Society of India, and was made a member of a committee to investigate for the Government various plans
for the planting of new forests, and maintenance of
those already in existence.

By now he was becoming known in many parts of
the world; naturalists and other friends were sufficiently interested to collect natural history specimens
for his collection, and these he added to the museum
he was forming.

More than once his garden suffered from the
elements and much of it was washed away, but with
tremendous vigour he set about the replanting to bring
it up again to its original beauty.

Through the years his garden increasingly became
his favourite sanctuary. Here he could be alone for his
quiet times. He could rest awhile, appreciating afresh
the Bible verse: 'Be still and know that I am God'
(Psalm 46:10). To the often weary pioneer it was a
temple where the very flowers spoke to him of their

Creator's love.

But even for the energetic Carey, there came a time when in the very nature of things he knew he must slow down. He had passed the allotted span.

> Returning birthdays tend to make us old
> But in their passing leave their dust of gold.
> Which taken up by God's refining hand
> Can yet accomplish all that he has planned.

The fever which attacked him repeatedly left its legacy too, and by 1833 it became noticeable that his strength was failing. At last the day came when he could no longer walk around his garden and this fact distressed him so much that his friends determined to find some solution. They fixed a chair on to a board fitted with four wheels, and on this Emmett-like contraption he was drawn along the paths each day.

'Go slowly, friend,' he would say to the person wheeling his chariot. 'Take me near the flowers so that I can smell their fragrances. Close enough to see again their beauty.'

Eventually, even these trips became an impossibility through increasing weakness, but his interest remained as keen as ever. He insisted on the gardeners coming to his room so that he could discuss with them details for the future of his plants and give them necessary instructions.

The proofs of his final revision of the Bengali New Testament arrived from the printers and Carey spent his remaining days reading these.

He was greatly cheered by news from England of renewed confidence in the Mission and new support for the work to continue. Marshman was with him when he received the letter and with a deep sigh of relief Carey looked across the table at his friend and colleague. 'This makes my cup not only full but running over,' he said. 'There is nothing more left in this world for me to wish for.'

Lady Bentinck and the Bishop of Calcutta were among the many friends who called to see him. One of the last was Alexander Duff, who had never forgotten the kind welcome and encouragement Carey had given him when he discussed those early plans for an educational mission. He spoke glowingly of this now to the old veteran who accepted the man's appreciative remarks with his usual spirit of humility.

When the time came for his visitor to leave he said softly: 'Mr Duff, you have been talking much of Dr Carey. When I am gone, say nothing about Carey. Speak instead of Carey's Saviour.'

As the sun rose into a cloudless sky on the morning of June 9th, 1834 the pioneer reached the last rung of the ladder. As he entered into the eternal presence of the Author, in his hand was the new edition of the Bengali New Testament.

India had said goodbye to one of her greatest benefactors, and on the Danish Government House at Serampore the flag was seen to be flying at half-mast.

27

'Dust of Gold'

Serampore is known as the cradle of modern missions in the East, and this college that William Carey founded is still a part of India's culture. But it is not the only memorial to this great missionary pioneer, translator, professor and preacher.

No one could have foreseen the lasting result of the tremendous impact his *Enquiry* made on the Protestant churches of his day. This unique document proved to be a vital landmark in the history of missionary enterprise, presenting as it did a challenge to Christians and reminding them of their responsibility to the peoples of other lands. Through the years many other societies have been formed as a result of the founding of that first Baptist Society.

Some of the gathered 'dust of gold' from Carey's life can be seen today in the Carey Library which the Serampore Triad set up in 1800 and which, by the middle of the 19th century, had been reorganized to become one of the most valuable libraries in India.

In 1961 a Carey Museum was formed at Serampore,

attached to the library, and this holds a collection of precious manuscripts, books, pamphlets, periodicals and other reading materials in 101 languages— Oriental and European. Most of the articles were collected by the early missionaries, and there are polyglot dictionaries and vocabularies, many published by them.

Bibles naturally have an important place and these are written in thirty-four Asian and forty-three European languages.

Among the scientific articles are those depicting the Mission's pioneering endeavour to introduce science education, and another interesting exhibit is a copy of the Royal Charter granted by the Danish King to establish Serampore as Asia's first university.

There are important monuments in the museum, including a pair of staircases and the original gates of iron from the front of the building, which were a gift of King Frederick VI.

Among the personal belongings of Carey are his desk, letter-box, pen, crutches used in later life, medicine chest, spectacles, and pulpit. On the desk is the daily account book of the Serampore Mission family, a valuable and interesting record of housekeeping in a community setting at the beginning of the 19th century.

The museum is part of the college and its administration is supervised by a member of the staff who acts as Honorary-in-charge.

The college, now under the auspices of the Baptist Missionary Society, still functions in the old building which Carey built, but has grown considerably. Today there are some sixty theological students, most of them working for a Bachelor of Divinity degree. They come from many parts of India and their common language is English.

In accordance with the original vision of its founder, Serampore is also an Arts and Science College, and these students are mainly local, often coming straight from school. The language used is Bengali.

On the other side of the world the City of Leicester which said goodbye to William Carey in 1793 has, in the 20th century, welcomed many Asian people into its midst to become part of its social life, its industry and its future history.

But the missionary pioneer would hardly recognize the city he left, for the face of Leicester is ever changing as modern schemes develop. When, halfway through this century, Harvey Lane and its Baptist Chapel disappeared in the wake of the bulldozer, the City Council planned to spare Carey's cottage and keep it as a memorial to the one-time cobbler.

But in 1968 progress had its unrelenting way, and in April of that year the demolition squad moved in. The humble cottage crumbled into dust to make way for the new Southgate underpass. Bricks and Swithland slates from the building were sold to souvenir hunters, and Leicester lost an important heritage.

Carey Close, the name given to the widened road where the cottage once stood, is the only reminder to those who pass by of one of Leicester's most remarkable citizens.

More important than the relics, is the fact that the work Carey began goes on today. In August 1983 a London newspaper carried this headline '*Asian Anglicans buy own church*'. This was in the city of Birmingham, the heart of the English Midlands. The

report stated that most of the congregation came origi-
nally from the Punjab, and the members wish to
preserve their own cultural identity while continuing
to be within the church. The service is conducted in a
mixture of English, Urdu and Bengali, and the
minister preaches in whatever is the dominant language among those listening.

Jesus said: 'Go therefore and make disciples of all
nations' (Matthew 28:19, Revised Standard Version).
He also said: 'And men will come from east and west,
and from north and south, and sit at table in the
kingdom of God' (Luke 13:29, Revised Standard
Version).

It was in those promises that William Carey put his
trust as he attempted great things for God.